New and Selected Poems
of
Patrick Galvin

New and Selected Poems

of

Patrick Galvin

edited by

Greg Delanty and Robert Welch

CORK UNIVERSITY PRESS

First published in 1996 by
Cork University Press
University College
Cork
Ireland

The previously published poems in this collection first appeared in *Heart of Grace* (Linden Press, London, 1959), *Christ in London* (Linden Press, London, 1960), *The Wood Burners* (New Writers' Press, Dublin, 1973), *Man on the Porch* (Martin, Brian and O'Keefe, London, 1979) and *Folk Tales for the General* (Raven Arts Press, Dublin, 1989).

British Library Cataloguing in Publication Data
A CIP catalogue record for this book is available from
the British Library.

ISBN 1 85918 079 5 h/b
     1 85918 091 4 p/b

Typeset by Tower Books of Ballincollig, Co. Cork
Printed by ColourBooks of Baldoyle, Co. Dublin

Contents

Introduction by Greg Delanty and Robert Welch vii
Biography xvii

New Poems
Poem for my Last Birthday 3
Only the Mad 4
The Girls of Pontevedra 5
Song for Angelica 6
For One Who Disappeared 7

Folk Tales for the General (1989)
My Father Spoke with Swans 11
Nothing is Safe 13
The Perfect Bar of Soap 14
Captain Titan 15
The Man Who Burns Poems 17
Last Death of the Evening 19
Roses for the President 22
Incident at Oviedo 23
Folk Tale for the General 25
The Oldest Man in Gernika 28
The Wall 31
Lobster Pots 33
McDonagh's Wife 35

Man on the Porch (1979)
Man on the Porch 41
Advice to a Poet 43
Plaisir d'Amour 44
Prisoners of the Tower 47
The Cage 50
Midnight 51
Testament 55
Message to the Editor 58

The Wood Burners (1973)

The Wood Burners 63
Miss Cecily Finch 65
The Madwoman of Cork 67
The Leopard 70
Birthday 71
David Gleeson 72
Statement on the Burning of Cork 73
Loving 77
Dispossessed 79
Lochan 80

Christ in London (1960)

Song for a Poor Boy 87
from Roxy's
Prologue 89
1 Roxy's 90
2 First Confession 91
4 Lackery 93
5 Remember the Night? 94
6 The Stag 96
7 The Kings are Out 97
Christ in London 101

Heart of Grace (1959)

My Little Red Knife 111
An Caisideach Bán 112
The White Monument 114
Madasha 119
A Day of Rebellion 121
Chicken Coop 127

Notes 129

Introduction

... my father was talking to Pyramid Reilly. He was another expert. He'd studied the Pyramids of Egypt for years and could now prove, beyond doubt, that the Lost Tribes of Israel were living in Evergreen Street.

Patrick Galvin, *Song for a Poor Boy* (1990)

Patrick Galvin was born on 15 August 1927 at 13 Margaret Street, Cork. The house no longer exists, having been pulled down some years ago. Galvin's own comment is (letter to the editors 17 April 1996): 'It should have been blown up in 1927'. It was a desperately poor area, but it was a very old part of Cork City, that highly atmospheric locale between St Finnbarre's Church of Ireland Cathedral and Evergreen Road. Barrack Street climbs up from the flat of the city to become the Bandon Road; to each side are French's Quay and Sullivan's Quay; and between the quays and Beamish and Crawford's brewery there extends the old South Gate Bridge, a bridge taking its name from one of the gates in the old (now mostly gone) city wall. Behind this long river front, outside the old city, there was a labyrinth of inter-connecting thoroughfares, sometimes scarcely a yard across, climbing up the hill to Greenmount. To this day these streets, alleyways, laneways, bridges, teem with life: there are cake shops, grocers, haberdasheries, wool shops, pork butchers, greengrocers; there is a slapdash, slightly improvised air about the establishments, all, that is, apart from the pubs, of which there are a great number, with their opaque frosted windows, discreet-looking varnished doors, and the invitingly sour smell of beer and stout. There is incessant talk and busy-ness; greetings and *badinage* are shouted from one side of the street to the other; a young woman dressed to kill walks by, drawing exclamations of exquisite pain from young lads outside a newsagent's, having a smoke before they return to school. Back in the early 1930s the scene would not in essence be that different: more of the streets would be cobbled; the men and women would be paler because of poorer nourishment; the children would be dirtier; and there would be no traffic, apart from horse drays, bicycles, handcarts. The smells would be stronger, perhaps. But then, as now, the Lee would flow slowly under the South Gate Bridge, a thick oily green ooze, carrying the detritus of the city to Cork Harbour and the open sea.

The city in which Galvin grew up in the 1930s, as he tells us in the trilogy of autobiographies, *Song for a Poor Boy* (1990), *Song for a Raggy Boy* (1991) and *Song for a Fly Boy* (due 1997), was one that had an immense vitality and social energy. In many ways its culture was a semi-literate one; or, to put it another way, it still retained many of the features of oral culture. Galvin's (admittedly to some degree fictionalized and perhaps slightly romanticized) autobiographies are crowded with storytellers, characters of abrupt and sudden impulses, eccentrics, sailors, old soldiers, romancers, dreamers. However, allowing for the rosy tinge that affectionate backward perspectives can introduce, it is evident that 'inner city' Cork of the 1930s was a place animated by a folk culture of remarkable richness. It had the cultural community of a harbour city, which had absorbed so many influences in its thousand-year-long history: Danes, Normans, English, Huguenots, Welsh and Dutch. Its language retained (still retains) guttural 'rs' from French, and even a Scandinavian 'v' in 'tiv', a version of the preposition 'to' in Standard English; but aside from these survivals there is a flourish and speed in Cork Hiberno-English that make it an eloquently expressive medium, particularly for the purposes of derision and abuse. Cork Hiberno-English is further enlivened, however, by another language and culture that came with the people who settled, mostly, *outside* the city gates, whether up Barrack Street and Sullivan's Quay and Mary Street to the south; or up Shandon Street and Blarney Street and Eason's Avenue to the north. These were the Irish, the Gaelic-speaking landless people, drawn to the city for work and opportunity, from a land where, quite often, they were leaving circumstances of appalling hardship and poverty. They brought with them the stories, customs, beliefs, practices, and mind-set of the Gaelic world. Mixing with the life of the city, and stimulated by its difference and the sense of human excitement people living in large groups create, a new culture was created, an amalgam of all the elements that went into the making of the city's life, including, most crucially, and permeating all, the Gaelic element. This presence, transposing itself to accommodate to a new language and a new environment, gives to Cork's language, in speech, declamation, song or poetry, a tang of abrupt otherness, the tug of a different grammar: 'he have no shame'; 'would you look at your wan in that rigout'; 'he does be always at the pub around four'. The present writers are no linguists, and these examples are taken at random, but it is evident that syntax, grammar, and, crucially, verb-formation draw upon Irish. In this, Cork Hiberno-English is not, of course, different from the Hiberno-English of other parts of Ireland. Where Cork does differ is that as a relatively small city with a tenacious and established English-speaking mercantile class, itself containing a variety of other continental influences, it offered an example of cultural and linguistic interaction with Gaelic society and language over hundreds of years. Dublin was cushioned, to some extent, from this influence by the existence of the Pale around the city; and Belfast, when it began to expand as an industrial centre in the 1800s, had already begun to regard itself as distinct from its Gaelic and Catholic hinterlands for political and sectarian reasons. In Cork, as perhaps in Waterford, there was more give and take, and this is reflected in the easy confident tenor of life in that city, its (often infuriating) self-assurance, and its conviction (surely not entirely without foundation) that it is like nowhere else on earth. This animatedness, reflected in the linguistic richness of Cork speech, is the background for the vitality that continually surfaces in Galvin's poetry, prose, and songs. And it is a vitality that roots itself in a complex interplay of variant cultural traditions.

One example of that mixed inheritance is Galvin's well-known poem, 'The Madwoman of Cork'. It is an example of declamation: speech driven by passion as the woman in the poem tries, vehemently, to give vent to her mixture of vision and rage. Yeats wrote a series of poems, The Crazy Jane sequence, with a similar kind of inspiration – the figure of the woman liberated from the constraints of society, saying outrageous and passionate things, a rebuke to the lives of those who shroud instinct and corral emotion – but Galvin's woman has a rawer, more tumultuous energy. 'The Madwoman of Cork' is connected to the semi-oracular, semi-prophetic outpourings of the 'prophecy-men' and '-women' who were a feature of the Irish countryside and small towns in the eighteenth and nineteenth centuries, and depicted (gloomily) in William Carleton's *The Black Prophet* (1847). Galvin's woman has the power to 'see things':

> Yesterday
> In Castle Street
> I saw two goblins at my feet
> I saw a horse without a head
> Carrying the dead
> To the graveyard
> Near Turner's Cross.

Galvin conveys, in powerful images, a piety and religious devotion of consuming strength, even though the constraints of reason have given way, and vision crosses over into nightmare:

When Canon Murphy died
I wept on his grave
That was twenty-five years ago.
When I saw him just now
In Dunbar Street
He had clay in his teeth.
He blest me.

This makes for strong poetry out of the interplay between religion's established forms ('Canon Murphy') and a pagan and Celtic intimation that life and death cross over into one another, a feature of Irish folk culture, in city and country.

But behind this oracular declaration, and its sharp, almost surrealist, imagery, there lies a yet older formation, one of the oldest in Irish literature, legend, and myth: the figure of the 'cailleach' or hag. Galvin is quite aware of this, of course, because he draws upon one of the most complete and effective expressions of this archetype in the literature, 'The Old Woman of Beare' in the following stanza:

I should like to be young
To dress up in silk
And have nine children.
I'd like to have red lips
But I'm eighty years old.
I have nothing
But a small house with no windows.

Compare this with the ninth-century poem:

I am the Hag of Beare
I once wore a shirt that was always new,
Today I have become so thin
That I would not wear out even an old shirt.

Galvin's treatment of this figure is influenced by her manifestations in literature, not just in the Old Irish version (which he would have known probably in Frank O'Connor's translation) but also in those of Yeats (Crazy Jane) and Austin Clarke ('The Young Woman of Beare'); however, Galvin's poem restores her to a context in the oral culture of Gaelic and English-speaking Ireland. This renewal of her demotic energy allows him to create subtle and strikingly modern effects in imagery and rhythm.

A further dimension of this poem is the sense it gives of a concern for the casualties of society. A social, indeed socialist, impulse animates the imaginative life he creates for his archetypal figure, and this active conscience is frequently evident in Galvin's writings, leading him, on occasion, to sermonizing and opinion-making. However, in his best writings the demotic force of his language carries an utterly democratic impetus, a sense that society ultimately must rest upon sharing, mutuality, concern.

Galvin's political convictions were forged out of a variety of influences, and among these, a particular importance may be attached to the self-respect and fraternal pride that was fostered in the nineteenth-century craftsmens' and artisans' guilds in Cork. There was a sense of the dignity and pride of labour, and of course good craftsmen were in demand in a successful mercantile, trading, and manufacturing city that acted as the supplying harbour for ocean-going ships heading for the Americas. The rights of the skilled craftsmen were jealously protected in this context of economic prosperity, which meant that there was a hierarchy of labour and that a sense of value was attached to physical work. Cork had (still has?) a working class not easily cowed and one keenly concerned with issues of social justice. This is one reason why Jews were welcome in Cork in the early twentieth century, when other cities adopted distinctly anti-semitic attitudes. The small but very significant Jewish population of Cork surfaces in Galvin's autobiographical writings in a hatred of fascist, totalitarian and authoritarian ideologies, which is everywhere in evidence in his poetry and drama.

The most formative influence, however, on Galvin's radical liberalism was the fact that he grew up in a city with a tradition of rebellion after the Anglo-Irish war of 1919–22 won partial independence for Ireland from Britain. There was much disillusionment, and that mood informs the atmosphere of the post-revolutionary school of realist prose, chief among which was that of the Corkmen Frank O'Connor and Sean O'Faolain. But there was also hope, anticipation, and not a little patriotic pride among ordinary people, in spite of the funnelling away of energies that censorship and the advanced clericalism of a reinvigorated Irish Catholicism represented. Certainly the spirit of Connolly's humane socialism informed Galvin's boyhood and early manhood as much as the sacral transcendentalism of Patrick Pearse.

However, the figure of Michael Collins, IRA leader and one of the chief negotiators of the Treaty, haunted Galvin's imagination, as it did that of many young men in Cork and the rest of Ireland in the post-revolutionary period. His ruthlessness, integrity and daring, and the fact that he was ambushed and killed in mysterious circumstances made him a figure of mystery and power, qualities celebrated in Galvin's lament for the 'Big Fella' in 'The White Monument':

In the evening we buried him
We raised him on our shoulders
And walked with him to Douglas.
And the windows draped in seaweed
And the streets filled with iron ghosts
The blood grew hard upon the road
And we buried him.

This poem is trying to create a grand 'monumental' gesture of great loss at the disappearance of an invigorating energy (Collins's) out of communal Irish life. The poet is seeking to be, as the Gaelic folk poet frequently was, a voice for a social sorrow. It is a *caoineadh*, owing something to the laments of Raftery from Connacht and Eibhlín Dubh Ní Chonaill's lament for her husband Art O'Leary. Once again the social and socialist (in the broadest sense) impulse is in evidence.

But another element creeps in as well, and a crucial and determining one in Galvin's array of voices: it is a note of excited celebration that comes from Federico García Lorca. Galvin learnt from Lorca how it was possible to unite folk energy with modernist and indeed surrealist effects. This alliance is bravely attempted in 'The White Monument', when the Irish *caoineadh* and Lorca's lyrical enthusiasm are joined to evoke and salute the chthonic power and vital masculinity of Michael Collins. Somewhere behind the Collins poem is Lorca's great lament for his friend, a bullfighter, 'Llanto por la muerte de Ignacio Sanchez Mejias' (1934), and indeed bull-imagery features prominently in 'The White Monument'. Galvin's poem has great exuberance and invention (the surrealistic seaweed draped in the windows; the iron ghosts on the streets) but it finally doesn't realize its own ambitions, partly because, perhaps, modern English cannot sustain a long note of excited elegy in the way Irish and Spanish can. We find it hard to take, and yet it is a piece of great originality, which tries for registers of feeling and surprising collocations of emotion and image strange to Irish poetry in the 1950s (when the poem was written) but more familiar to us now through the exercises in surrealistic perspectives and bizarre tones undertaken by Paul Durcan and Gerry Murphy, each of whom learned a good deal from Galvin's own methods. And they too, like Galvin, use surrealist effects partly to awaken a moribund social conscience.

Galvin has studied the tonality and moods of Gaelic poetry, as his versions of Seán Ó Murchadha na Ráithíneach and Tomás Ó Casaíde ('David Gleeson' and 'An Caisideach Bán') make clear, as well as his adaptation of the Hag of Beare poem in 'The Madwoman of Cork'. The long poem 'Lochan' makes use of Irish dinnsheanchas tradition (which transmitted the lore attached to places from one generation to the next) to create a quasi-mythical lament for the dispossession of the native Irish from their lands in and around Cork. He brings together the oracular force accorded poetry in ancient Irish divinatory lore with shocking and arresting imagery to create a disturbing piece which gives an edge to anger in the rhetorical fire:

> Lochan's coffin I stole from Gill Abbey Rock
> His bones wrapped in pure silver.
>
> When I die
> Say for me a Mass of the Lances.

The poet has also written songs and ballads (the famous 'James Connolly', so well-known in the version by Christy Moore, is his), and has made seven LP records. He is, in other words, working entirely from within the tradition of Irish folk song in English, while also fully alive to its Gaelic antecedents and influences. But what transforms this inheritance is his ability to introduce another element, a charge of risk, danger, and surprise. This owes something to his study of Lorca, something to his reflections upon and (ultimately) his refusal of the Yeatsian model of the isolated imagination in conflict with history. But at the end of the day (and this is where Galvin's interest as a poet most surely resides) there is something mysteriously 'Galvinesque' about this quality of danger and excess. He is a poet of the troubled conscience, and many (especially later) poems, such as 'Folk Tales for the General' bear generous witness to this; however, there is another Galvin which is wonderfully indifferent to conscience and its troubles. This is the one we see traces of in 'The White Monument', which celebrates the sheer energy, beyond our judgement, of a powerful personality. But it is thrillingly present in that superb piece of insouciant brilliance, 'My Little Red Knife'. This is a poem out for trouble, and loving every minute of it:

> With my little red knife
> I met my love
> With my little red knife
> I courted
> And she stole me to her deep down bed
> Her hair spread out a burning red
> But never a single word was said
> About my little red knife.

Nothing as daring had happened in Irish poetry since the wildness of Yeats in the mid 1930s. This was the real thing. And in the long sequence 'Roxy's' all Galvin's variant voices – ballad, Gaelic satire, parody, surrealistic juxtapositions, demotic power, social awareness – come together in a hymn to the particular energy of city life in Cork. In interviews with Greg Delanty, conducted in June and September of 1995, Galvin said that the sequence of poems 'is about the abuse of power', and that is certainly the case:

> They gouged out the eyes
> And they murdered the lips
> And they buried the tongue
> And the voice in the vile eclipses.

The 'Kings' and 'Queens' of this poem are figures of brazen authority, trampling the weak underfoot. All very well. But, and it is here that the 'Galvinesque' energy resides, there is also a sense that the poem celebrates energy, no matter where it comes from or what it does as long as it proclaims itself as what it is, without pretence or posturing. When one reads

> In Patrick Street
> In Grattan Street
> The Kings are out

something not quite licit gloriously stirs. Robert Welch recalls Seán Lucy, Galvin's friend and editor, reading these lines in that high, strong, delicate voice of his, as part of his first-year lecture series on the language of poetry, and the lecture theatre was ravished:

> Along the Mall
> The Union Quay
> In every street along the Lee
> The Kings are out.

> With knives of ice
> And dressed to kill
> The wine flows down from Summer Hill
> Christ! be on your guard tonight
> The Kings are out.

This carries its own authority because it is unstinting in its praise for and delight in the movement of life. It may be terrible, but in its own way it is also a marvellous thing that the 'Kings', in all their unstoppable force, are 'out'.

Galvin's later poetry reflects his experiences in Northern Ireland, where he went to live in 1973 to take up a post as writer-in-residence in the Lyric Theatre in Belfast. Others have written poems about the 'Troubles' in the North, but very few have written with the immediacy and directness to be found in, for example, 'Midnight'. In poems such as this, and in others not explicitly to do with the 'Troubles' ('Message to the Editor'), we encounter a poetry of the appalled conscience. The social awareness of the early poetry and the presence in it of a surrealist disruption of established modes of perception have fanned out into a kind of civilized anarchic pessimism about the tireless angers of men as they jostle for supremacy in a world of diminishing resources. The chthonic energies of the Kings and Queens have disappeared, and in their stead Galvin has assumed the role of jestful, if somewhat gloomy fabulist, as in 'Roses for the President'.

In the mood of a Pablo Neruda or a Gabriel García Márquez, an enigmatic situation is evolved in a kind of skeletal folk tale. There was some incident, involving a girl, which took place in a square; there were roses; there was a protest of some kind; there was an execution. All this is swiftly sketched in, as well as the president's failure to recall exactly what he did, and what the whole thing was about. The poem evokes the political amnesia and the anxieties of late capitalist power, but also its brutality and unpredictability. The poem also hints that contemporary arguments – that everything comes down to language, that identity is a constructed thing, that there may be no central meaning to anything, even the personality itself – collude with the expansion of cruelty and raw power:

> Of course, that particular incident
> May not have taken place at all.
> Have you considered that?
> So many things are illusory –
> The keening of snow
> The endless dreamings of the heart.

This president is capable of executing people in the square, even the girl he loved, but he is also quite a sophisticated exponent of philosophical and moral relativism. You might say that such a position helps brutality, just as it helps to be a sentimentalist:

> When I die, the President declared,
> Lay me out in the garden
> So that I may taste the roses.

The sentimentalist can enjoy the largesse of his own fine feelings and let the rest of the world go hang.

It will be evident that there is, in Galvin's later poetry, a deep distrust of language itself. He cuts away image, metaphor, rhythm, to concentrate on the matter at hand. It is a committed poetry, but committed to direct statement. It is not a method that is very common in Irish or English tradition, although it is now made more use of as contemporary activist movements seek to express their views in terse forms. There is, however, a problem, in that the poetry of direct statement often relies for its force on what it is making the statement about, and the political or moral value being advanced. Whether this always functions as poetry, which has its own distinct imaginative life and its own (not always amenable) energies, is a difficult matter to resolve.

Galvin is a poet who combines a very strong sense of the community that shaped and formed him, and gave him his voice, with a broad set of human concerns, that range from social idealism through pity for the victims of power, to anger at wrongs done. In spite of this alert and engaged conscience, however, his verse also celebrates that energy which is indifferent to our moral and conscientious objections. He is excited by the Blakean tiger. He can be a surrealist, an enigmatic fabulist, and can write poetry charged with his own unique view of the world. In spite of the doubts about language that surface in his later poems the strength of his verse lies in the sense of urgency it creates, that something must be said and said with force.

Greg Delanty
Robert Welch

Biography

> I'm delighted to provide you with the biographical details you require – up to a point! This is not due to any mania for secrecy on my part, but simply because anything that I wish to reveal about my life is contained in my published work . . .
>
> (Patrick Galvin, letter to the editors, 17 April 1996)

1927:   Born at 13 Margaret St, Cork, 15 August.

1934:   Attended South Presentation Convent School. Sold broad-sheets of sheet songs and ballads in the streets after school, and in pubs at night, reciting them from bar counters when required.

1935?:   Family moved to 5 Coyle's Square, Evergreen St.

1939:   Left school under age (he should have been fourteen) by having a birth certificate altered by a master-forger in Barrack St for a half-crown. Began working as a messenger boy, newspaper boy, then as a projectionist in the Washington St Cinema ('The Washa'); also worked at the Lee Cinema, Winthrop St.

1943:   Went to Belfast intending to join the American Air Force, but enlisted in the RAF instead, again under age. Served with Bomber Command in the UK and Middle East, and with Coastal Command in Africa. Saw the bombed cities of Europe shortly after VE Day.

1949?:   London, various jobs; hitch-hiked around Europe.

1950?:   Began writing poetry.

1953?–1959:   Met Séamus Ennis, the traditional uilleann piper, who encouraged him as a folk-singer. Made some EP records for WMA (Workers' Music Association, now Topic Records). Later made seven LPs for Stinson Records, New York, then Riverside Records, also New York.

1959:   *Heart of Grace* (Linden Press, London). 'Life and Poetry of J.M. Synge' (Radio Feature, BBC 3).

1960:   *Christ in London* (Linden Press, London).

1962:   Moved to Dublin. *And Him Stretched* (play, Unity Theatre, London).

1963:   *Cry the Believers* (play, Eblana Theatre, Dublin). Returned to London.

1965:   *Boy in the Smoke* (TV play, BBC 2). Returned to Ireland, living at Roaring Water Bay, West Cork.

1967–69:   Visited Spain, Israel, Germany. Returned to Ireland.

1973:   *The Wood Burners* (New Writers' Press, Dublin). Leverhulme Fellowship in Drama, and resident dramatist at Belfast's Lyric Theatre (1974–77). *Nightfall To Belfast* (play, Lyric).

1974:   Directed *Purgatory* by W.B. Yeats (Lyric). *The Last Burning* (play, Lyric).

1975:   *We Do it for Love* (play, Lyric).

1976:   *The Devil's Own People* (play, Dublin Theatre Festival). *Three Plays* (Threshold Publications, Belfast).

1979:   *Man On the Porch: Selected Poems* (Martin Brian and O'Keefe, London). Lived in Spain for six months.

1980–81:   *Class Of '39* (radio play, BBC 4). Resident writer, East Midlands Arts (Mansfield, Notts). Read and recorded work at Library of Congress, Washington, DC. Returned to Belfast. *My Silver Bird* (play, with music by Peadar O'Riada, Lyric).

1982:   Wrote and directed *I Mind the Time* (One man show, Belfast Festival). Directed *Krapps Last Tape* by Samuel Beckett (Belfast Festival). Devised and directed *Bessie Smith* (Belfast Folk and Jazz Festival).

1983:   Research work in Spain. Returned to Ireland, Ballycotton, East Cork. *City Child Come Trailing Home* (radio play, RTÉ). *Landscape and Seascape* (radio play, RTÉ).

1984:   Elected to Aosdana. *Quartet for Nightown* (radio play, RTÉ). *Wolfe* (radio play, RTÉ).

1986:   Returned to Belfast. Adapted *The Country Woman* by Paul Smith (BBC 4). Adapted *The Monkey's Paw* by W. Jacobs (BBC 4 and World Service).

1987:   Directed *Oscar Wilde* (Brighton Pavilion).

1989:   *Folk Tales for the General* (Raven Arts, Dublin).

1990:   *Song for a Poor Boy* (Raven Arts, Dublin).

1991:   Reading tour in Mexico and Newfoundland. Returned to Cork city. *Song for a Raggy Boy* (Raven Arts, Dublin).

1994:	*The Death of Art O'Leary* (Three Spires Press, Cork). O'Shaughnessy Award for Poetry (Irish American Cultural Institute). Reading tour in America.
1995:	Resident writer, Dún Laoghaire–Rathdown County Council.
1996:	Edited *Dún Laoghaire–Rathdown County Anthology*, containing extracts from *Village Diary*, a phantasmagoric fiction in short scenes by Galvin.

New Poems

Poem for my Last Birthday

I'd be a better bard
Had I known the ins and outs of things
But I was never sure which side I was on.

When I heard clerics intoning
Through the mouths of cows
I longed for a bolt of lightning
To poke them up the jowls.
Or better still – an earthquake
To upheave the bowels.

What I should have done
Was join the cows
Issuing miracles of milk
To cure the sick,
The blind, the maimed
And the cleric's hole.

Instead,
I stood there gawking
Until some gobshite would say –
'Will you look at that?
What kind of people are they at all?'

It was then that all those humanitarian clichés
Came sparkling out of the bag:
'People are entitled to their beliefs';
And – 'Aren't they better off doing that
Than playing with guns?'

O God!
O Druids!
O circle of stones!
Pardon my ambiguities
Pity my iniquities
And comfort me

During
These long hours
Of darkening revolutions.

Only the Mad

Only the mad live here
Those who paint mirrors on the wall
And rage at their own reflection.

If
You look closely
You will see that these people
Have no heads.
You may also observe
That they have no feet.
If they had
They would walk out of here.

As for myself
I lost my eyes yesterday.
I plucked them out
Bottled them in brine
And then the bottle disappeared.
That's the kind of thing
That happens here –
Thieves everywhere.

But what of you?
You've eaten your tongue
I could feel that.
I heard the noise you made
And it was most unpleasant.
But what about the rest of you?
Have you screamed yet?
That's normal.

Only the mad live here
Those who paint mirrors on the wall
And rage at their own reflection.

The Girls of Pontevedra

The girls of Pontevedra
Stood close to the water
And in the sunlight of the reeds
The boys played Holy Communion.

When Jesus walked on the water
The girls followed him
But the boys remained
Hidden in the reeds
And blest with Holy Communion.

When Jesus died on the water
It was said that the waves
Failed to anoint him
And when the girls died
On the water
It was said that Jesus failed
To uplift them.

Only the boys survived
Naked in the reeds
Entwined forever in games
Of Holy Communion.

Song for Angelica

My child is a stone tree
Glowing in Honduras.
I send her the colour green
She sends me a flower
Fresh from an underground lake.

My child is a still poem
Sounding in Honduras.
I send her the colour blue
She sends me the moon
And the image of a barred gate.

My child is a dark voice
Silent in Honduras.
I send her the colour red
She sends me a storm
Painted on the walls of her cell.

For One Who Disappeared

Do you remember Christmas
Do you remember the snow
The child in the window
The unrelenting sea
Do you remember me?

2

The snow whispers at Christmas.
It lingers down night corners
It listens on the telephone
It opens doors
And then closes them again.

3

People disappear at Christmas
They become snow rivers
Nameless
Unborn
The snow buries them.

4

The moon bleeds at Christmas
The child withers in white
The snow blossoms
Only the blind can see
Promises carved in the sun.

5

Do you remember Christmas
Do you remember the snow
The child in the window
The unrelenting sea –
Do you remember me?

Folk Tales for the General (1989)

r

My Father Spoke with Swans

Leaning on the parapet
Of the South Gate Bridge
My father spoke with swans
Remembering his days
With the Royal Munster Fusiliers.

India was dawn
The women cool
The sun cradled in his arms.
Sometimes,
When the clouds were wine
He washed his face in the Ganges.

The swans rose from the Lee
And held their wings.

2

Leaning on the mysteries
Of her twilight room
My mother spoke with God
Remembering Pearse
And the breath of Connolly.

Ireland was new
The men tall
The land mirrored their brightness.
Sometimes,
When the eagles called
She walked the roads to Bethlehem.

God opened his eyes
A loss for miracles.

From these two I was born
The Ganges swaying with the Lee
And gunfire rising to a fall.
My mother wore green till she died
My father died with swans.

Only the rivers remain
Slow bleeding.

Nothing is Safe

Nothing is safe anymore.
I wrote a poem last night
And when I woke up this morning
There was no sign of it.

I thought the mice had eaten it
(We're subject to mice in this house)
But then again
Why should they?
Poetry doesn't agree with mice.

Of course,
The present climate being
What it is
Anything may have happened –
A sudden rain storm
During the night
The cold air
Thieving through the window
And the poem dies of pneumonia.

Next time I write a poem
I'll send it to my aunt
Who lives in a madhouse.
She's blind
But she likes the texture of paper.
She holds it in her hand
Crinkles it up
And listens to the sound.

Perhaps
That's all that matters
In the end –
The sound of paper
Screaming in the hand.

The Perfect Bar of Soap

Whenever Pilate travelled on horseback
To foreign parts
He always carried in his saddle-bag
The perfect bar of soap –
And you could say
That he was simply preparing
For the inevitable.

But
Whether Pilate knew
What the inevitable was
Or where it would take place
Is another matter –
And where he obtained the soap
Has always been a mystery.

Recent discoveries,
However,
Have shown quite clearly
That the soap was a product
Of the only factory in Rome
To have paid its workers
At a very high rate.

It is not surprising
Therefore
That when Pilate washed his hands
Of the Jew
He walked away
Clean
As a whistle.

Captain Titan

Captain Titan walked on the water
He said he needed the exercise.

At the inquest, Mrs Titan said that she wasn't too surprised
to hear that her husband had been walking on the water. He
was always doing things like that – especially when he
had drink taken.

The Coroner nodded his head.
He understood perfectly –
The Captain was a seafaring man.

Last year, for example, the Captain had changed into a
seagull. Mrs Titan had no objections to seagulls. She rather
liked them, really. But the Captain's behaviour as a seagull
was quite outrageous. He insisted on flying in and out of the
village church and screeching for more fish.

The Coroner nodded his head.
He remembered the incident –
The Parish Priest was terrified.

The Captain was arrested for that little escapade and spent
three weeks in jail flapping his wings about and claiming
that under International Law it was illegal to imprison a
seagull. Mrs Titan knew nothing about International Law,
but she was convinced that the police could arrest anyone
for anything – even if he were a seagull.

The Coroner nodded his head.
He could see the headlines –
'Seagull sues police for wrongful arrest.'

Mrs Titan said she wasn't a bad wife. She'd tried hard to be
tolerant of the Captain and she was sorry now that she
hadn't understood him more. After all, there was nothing
wrong with being a seagull – and nothing wrong with
walking on the water either – if one had a mind to.

The Coroner summed up:
He said:
This is a tragic case.
He said:
I feel extremely sorry for the widow –
And offered to take her to lunch later
At the nearest seafood restaurant.

The Man Who Burns Poems

There's a man in this town
who burns poems.
I don't know his name
But every day I see smoke
Rising from the chimney
Of his house.

My wife says:
He's burning bodies.

Yesterday,
I saw the man who burns poems
Standing in our front garden.
He had a camera in his hand
And he was photographing
The dahlias.

My wife says:
He's looking for a place
To bury the ashes.

This morning
The man who burns poems
Knocked at our back door.
I refused to let him in
And he's been standing there
Ever since.

My wife says:
Wait until the rain falls –
Maybe it will wash him away.

I don't think
It's going to rain.
I think we're in for
A long hot millennium.
I'm going to eat my poems
And pretend I'm a seagull.

My wife says:
That should solve everything.

Last Death of the Evening

Earlier in the day
In what the police described
As yet another set
Of sectarian killings,
A young boy had been shot
In the Ormeau Road
And the body of a girl
Had been found in an alleyway
Along Murder Mile.

But these two
Were strangers to me
And their names
Fleeting on the radio
Meant nothing –
Two cyphers
On a digital clock.

The last death of the evening
Was different.

2

A friend
Republican to the core –
But no more –
His body lay on the pavement
Outside my door
His eyes open.

The bullet
Had entered the back
Of his head
And made its dum-dum
Exit
Through his ragged jaw.

I was surprised
He could still speak.
Help me
He said
For Christ's sake
Help me.

I tried
To staunch the wound
I tried
To freeze the blood
And I shouted for someone
To call a doctor.

But
The streets were empty
The curtains drawn
And Belfast had retreated
Behind its own
Fearful silence.

3

Presently
The army arrived
And presently
The doctor arrived
And presently
The police arrived at the death.

Did you witness
The killing?
Can you identify
The assailant?
From what direction
Was the bullet fired?

The blood eased
Its way
Along the pavement
And a policeman
Tried to circle it
With white chalk.

From a darkened doorway
A woman appeared –
She screamed
And a soldier shouted:
Tell that fucking woman
To shut up!

The woman ignored him
She ignored me.
She was staring at the circle
Of chalk
And she screamed
Maternally.

It was the last death
Of the evening.

Roses for the President

You may recall, Mr President,
The incident in the square.
Perhaps, you would tell us about that.

When I die, the President declared,
Lay me out in the garden
So that I may taste the roses.
I have always been partial to roses
And once knew a girl
Who wore nothing else.

I have forgotten her name
And I have no memory for faces
But I do remember the roses.

As to the incident in the square,
Which you have mentioned many times,
I have no recollection of that.
It was probably raining
And people protest, largely,
Because of the vagaries in the weather.

The roses smelled sweet
I remember that –
And she was remarkably tall.

Of course, that particular incident
May not have taken place at all.
Have you considered that?
So many things are illusory –
The keening of snow
The endless dreamings of the heart.

She lay face down in the rain
The roses covered her
I remember that.

Incident at Oviedo

Maria Luisa Fernandez
Set up her stall
In the market at Oviedo
And declared to the public
At large
That she was not a gypsy.

She sold needles and pins
Cottons and dyes
And iron pots –
But she was not,
She repeated again,
A common gypsy.

Her eight-year-old daughter,
Manuela, said nothing.
She stood close to her mother
Hand outstretched
Begging a peseta
From anyone who was interested.

When the policeman arrived
He demanded to see Maria's
Licence To Trade.
Maria had none –
And the policeman proceeded
To break up her stall.

It was then
That Maria Luisa Fernandez
Betrayed her origins –
She split the policeman
Over the head
With an iron pot.

The policeman, too
As befits his calling –
Revealed his origins.
He grabbed Maria by the hair
And dragged her off to
The nearest police station.

Maria's eight-year-old daughter,
Manuela, said nothing.
She remained motionless
Hand outstretched
Begging a peseta
From anyone who was interested.

A small yellow bird
Settled at her feet.
Manuela ignored it.

Folk Tale for the General

When the General died in his sleep
It rained everywhere
But the rifles,
Hidden in caves,
Smouldered a salute.

The General conceived
With the rifles.
He knew how to use them –
And when the General entered a room
The rifles stood to attention.

When the General looked in the mirror
The uniforms kissed him
And the medals
Pinned to his breast
Trembled with admiration.

The General appreciated things like that
They made him feel secure.

2

When the General was asked
About the guitars
He said he hated them
And spent his entire life
Killing them.

He said
The strings were like ropes
Round his neck
And the music a sword
In his ear.

He said
He was convinced
That people invented guitars.
Just to torment him
And he killed them too
And buried them
In heaps
In cemeteries without names.

3

When darkness fell
The General dreamed about guitars.
He could see them through walls,
In green corners
And under a multitude of beds.

But he screamed them out
Burned them into a daylight position
And when they were blind
He crushed them
Under a multitude of rifles.

Only then
Would he rest
Only then
Could he sleep without dreams
Only then would he die
Peacefully
And in communion
With God.

4

When the General died in his sleep
It rained everywhere.

Prisons of rain
Firing-squads of rain
Graveyards of rain
Crucifixions of rain
Falling.

And in the courtyards
Of the city
In the vineyards
And in the fields
The guitars
Took root
And blossomed
Fearfully.

The Oldest Man in Gernika

The oldest man in Gernika
Sat under the oldest oak tree
In Spain
And said:
Here, on this martyred green
Stood the oldest parliament
In the world.

The tourists threw pennies
At the tree
And the oldest man in Gernika
Nodded his head.
That will pay for the coffin
He said
But who will pay for the cross?

2

When the bombing began
The oldest man in Gernika
Was lying in bed.
He was thinking about his goats.

They gave the finest milk in Gernika,
He said
And when the land was burned
They were the first to die.

The oldest man in Gernika
Has been drinking
Black coffee
Ever since.

I do this in memory
He said.
I promised the goats
At the burial in Gernika.

3

When the artist, Garcia,
Drew a picture
Of the oldest oak tree in Spain
He omitted to include a portrait
Of the oldest man in Gernika

And
When the poster was published
In Gernika
It contained the words
Of the Basque National Anthem.

The oldest man in Gernika
Smiled.
That's as it should be,
He said.
The tree was there before me

And
The Basque National Anthem
Will be sung
Long after
I'm dead.

4

The tourists threw more pennies
At the tree
And one man purchased
A poster.

'Is this a Picasso?'
He asked –
And the oldest man in Gernika
Wept

Holy the ground
On which you stand
And holy the earth
That enfolds the Basque.

5

It was a pleasant day in Gernika
And the tourists enjoyed it immensely.

_ The Wall

The wall stood
In the village square
And no one knew
Who put it there or why.
It served no purpose
It belonged to no one
And it was built a mile away
From the sea.

You could measure our days
By the wall.

When a man died
We placed a stone on the wall
When a woman died
We placed two stones on the wall
And when a child died
We placed a small pebble on the wall
And you could feel
The bleeding.

You could measure our griefs
By the wall.

Sometimes,
We drew faces on the wall.
We carved our names on the wall
We drew small boats
Large fish
And storms at sea –
And one man painted
A lighthouse.

You could measure our lights
By the wall.

And
If you stood close to the wall
You could hear the Earth moving
The stars falling
And the sun sinking
Slowly
Into a folding sea.

You could measure our dark
By the wall.

—Broadcast RTE
(Well, a fiction
but was <u>built</u>
after)

Lobster Pots

The lobster
Is an edible decapod
With large claws
A curved fanlike tail
And stalked compound eyes.
You may eat the flesh.

Joanna
Sat at the edge of the pier
And dreamed of fish.

She liked fish.
Trout, certainly
And the occasional cut
Of pink salmon –
But not lobster.

Joanna
Didn't like lobster.

You had to boil them alive
For one thing
And then
There was that dreadful cracking
Of the shell.

Crabs
Were like that
And crayfish
And prawns
And shrimps.

Joanna
Didn't like them either.

Joanna
Stared at the lobster pots.
They were laid out
In neat rows
Against the sea wall
And they were empty.

She was glad about that
And relieved
To put it mildly
That she had never eaten
A lobster.

She preferred trout
And the occasional cut
Of pink salmon.

The lobster pot is a trap.
Sometimes,
The fishermen will place a mirror
In the pot
And the lobster is trapped
In the reflection of its own image.

McDonagh's Wife

McDonagh's body rose from the sea
Mrs McDonagh said nothing.

Being
Good neighbours
And decent people
We carried his body to the house
And laid it out on the kitchen table.
We felt it natural to mourn
But

Mrs McDonagh stared at the corpse
And said nothing.

At the graveside
We prayed for McDonagh's soul.
We placed flowers on his grave
And when the funeral was over
We raised a small headstone.
We felt that was the least we could do
But

Mrs McDonagh stood at the graveside
And said nothing.

Afterwards
We returned to McDonagh's house
For a drink
Or maybe something to eat –
That being the custom in these parts.
But the door lay closed to our faces
While

Mrs McDonagh sat at the window
And said nothing.

2

We retreated to the pub then
And drank a fist to McDonagh.
We praised his virtues
And condoned his faults.
A good man
Crossed by the waves
While

Mrs McDonagh settled at home
And said nothing.

We talked of other men –
Men like ourselves
Who worked hard
To keep a roof over their heads
While doleful women
Complained about nothing
And

Sent McDonagh and his like
To a watery grave.

3

We
Were glad when she left.
For London or New York
It makes no matter.

She
Wrote a letter from there.
Mailed it to the Parish Priest
And it was typical of her kind.

4

'I did not weep for McDonagh
Because I have wept enough
Through forty years of marriage.
I shall not weep again.

I bless the sea
I kiss the rising storm
I treasure the wave
That tumbled him to death.'

5

The Parish Priest
Threw her letter in the fire.
He did not understand
Women.

Man on the Porch (1979)

Man on the Porch

In the beginning

We didn't ask who he was
Or what he was doing there
On our front porch
Staring at us

But
You can take so much of a man
Who sits on the front porch
Staring at you

And in the end
We questioned him.

He made no answer.

We made food
Laid it out on a tray
In front of him
And it was good food

But he pushed it aside
And continued to sit there
On our front porch
Staring at us.

We thought he was mad
Or spoke a different language from us.

We made signs in the air.

We drew pictures on the ground
Friendly pictures
Of birds and animals
And lovers kissing under trees.

But
He said nothing
And made no mark
That he understood.

He just sat there on our front porch
Staring at us.

We thought we were mad.

We felt foolish
Standing there
Making signs in the air
And drawing pictures on the ground.

We told him to move.
It wasn't his front porch
It was ours
And we told him that

But he still sat there on our front porch
Staring at us

So we killed him.

We took him to our river
Tied two stones round his neck
And pushed him
Under the water.

We felt safer then –
For a time.

- Advice to a Poet

Be a chauffeur, my father said
And never mind the poetry.
That's all very well for the rich
They can afford it.
What you need is money in your belt
Free uniform and plenty of travel.
Besides that, there's nothing in verse.
And all poets are raging homosexuals.

I'd still like to be a poet.

Another thing: don't every marry
And if you do, then marry for cash.
Love, after all, is easily come by
And any old whore will dance for a pound.
Take my advice and be a chauffeur
The uniform will suit you a treat
Marriage and poems will blind you surely
And poets and lovers are doomed to hell.

I'd still like to be a poet.

But where's the sense in writing poetry?
Did any poet ever make good?
I never met one who wasn't a pauper
A prey to bailiffs, lawyers and priests.
Take my advice and be a chauffeur
With your appearance you're bound to do well
You might even meet some rich old widow
Who'll leave you a fortune the moment she dies.

I'd still like to be a poet.

Well, blast you then, your days are darkened
Poverty, misery, carnage and sin.
The poems you'll write won't be worth a penny.
And the women you marry will bleed you to death.
Take my advice and buy a revolver
Shoot yourself now in the back of the head.
The Government then might raise a subscription
To keep your poor father from breeding again.

Plaisir d'Amour

Spring

My father
Against the victories of age
Would not concede defeat
He dyed his hair
And when my mother called
He said he wasn't there.

My mother, too
Fought back against the years
But in her Sunday prayers
Apologised to God.
My father said there was no God
'And that one knows it to her painted toes.'

My mother smiled.
She'd plucked her eyebrows too
And wore a see-through skirt
With matching vest.
'He likes French knickers best,' she said
'I'll have them blest.'

My father raged.
He liked his women young, he said
And not half-dead.
He bought a second-hand guitar he couldn't play
And sang the only song he knew –
Plaisir d'Amour.

Summer

When summer came
My father left the house
He tied a ribbon in his hair
And wore a Kaftan dress.
My mother watched him walking down the street
'He'll break his neck in that,' she said –
'As if I care.'

He toured the world
And met a guru in Tibet.
'I've slept with women too,' he wrote
'And they not half my age.'
My mother threw his letter in the fire –
'The lying ghett – he couldn't climb the stairs
With all his years.'

She burned her bra
And wrote with lipstick on a card –
'I've got two sailors in the house
From Martinique.
They've got your children's eyes.'
My father didn't wait to answer that
He came back home.

And sitting by the fire
He said he'd lied
He'd never slept with anyone but her.
My mother said she'd never lied herself –
She'd thrown the sailors out an hour before he came.
My father's heart would never be the same –
Plaisir d'Amour.

Autumn

Through autumn days
My father felt the leaves
Burning in the corners of his mind.
My mother, who was younger by a year,
Looked young and fair.
The sailors from the port of Martinique
Had kissed her cheek.

He searched the house
And hidden in a trunk beneath the bed
My father found his second-hand guitar.
He found her see-through skirt
With matching vest.
'You wore French knickers once,' he said
'I liked them best.'

'I gave them all away,' my mother cried
'To sailors and to captains of the sea.
I'm not half-dead
I'm fit for any bed – including yours.'
She wore a sailor's cap
And danced around the room
While father strummed his second-hand guitar.

He made the bed,
He wore his Kaftan dress
A ribbon in his hair.
'I'll play it one more time,' he said
'And you can sing.'
She sang the only song they knew –
Plaisir d'Amour.

Winter

At sixty-four
My mother died
At sixty-five
My father.

Comment from a neighbour
Who was there:
'They'd pass for twenty.'
Plaisir d'Amour.

Prisoners of the Tower

I can see them now
Prisoners of the tower
Their faces blind
From centuries of barbed-wire.

If you are guilty
You know you are guilty
If you are innocent
You would not be here.

You are here
Therefore . . .

1

When the cell door closes
Behind you
You are free
When the cell door closes
Behind you
You are free
When the cell door closes
Behind you
You are free to weep
Endlessly
Without tears.

It is an offence
To shed tears in the tower
It is an offence
To grow old in the tower
It is an offence
To sit in the tower
But
You may walk freely
From wall to wall
And contemplate
The absence of bread.

Under our system of Government
A man has these rights:
You may walk freely from wall to wall
And contemplate the absence of bread.

2

You may not
Hear voices.

All prisoners
Who hear voices
Will report such voices
To the Keeper of the tower.
These voices do not exist
And if they do exist
They will be shot.
The shooting of voices
Is essential
To the harmony
Of the tower.

All prisoners
Who fail to report
The hearing of voices
Will be shot.
All prisoners
Who report the hearing of voices
Will be sent to a lunatic asylum.
Prisoners who are sent to a lunatic asylum
May
Lose the freedom of the tower
But the voices will stop.

Under our system of Government
A man has these rights:
You may lose the freedom of the tower
But the voices will stop.

3

You are free
To die.

All prisoners
Are entitled to death
All prisoners
Are entitled to a speedy death.
Any prisoner
Who is not capable of committing suicide
Will be shot
Any prisoner
Who fails to report
A desire to commit suicide
Will be shot.

When a prisoner dies in his cell
His body will remain in his cell.
It is an offence
To remove the dead from their cells.
It is assumed that in due time
Nature will corrupt the flesh
But the bones
If any
Remain the sole property of the prisoner.
He may return for these bones
At any time.

Under our system of Government
The dead also have rights:
You may return for these bones
At any time.

You are free
To have them.

The Cage

I think it's better to live in a cage
I mean, if you were free now
Free to walk about
You might step on a grave
And old men in shrouds would call you to account.

I think it's better to be blind
I mean, if you could see now
All that was happening here
You'd see smoke rising, leaves burning
And roots being cut.

I think it's better to be dumb
I mean, if you could speak now
Say what you wanted to
You'd say this was a police state,
That this nation was being sold to the lowest bidder.

I think it's better to live in a cage
It's quiet there and no one bothers you
And if you have dreams, nightmares,
Echoes in your mind of things past
And things to come

Then lose your mind
Pluck out your eyes
Rip out your tongue
And chop off your legs at the moving part
You're not going anywhere –

Are you?

Midnight

At midnight
At the first stroke of midnight
There was snow falling
On Antrim.
The wind had played
Upon the riverbeds
Since noon
But at midnight
The first stroke of midnight
It was lost among the reeds.

Then
It grew cold.
It was colder than it was
At any other time
Colder than ice
Colder than seven winters
Rolled into one
At midnight
The second stroke of midnight
Sounding in Antrim.

Listen now
To the third stroke of midnight –
A soldier stands in the street
A child cries in its mother's womb
A man opens his window
And looks out
At the snow falling
Gently
Over Antrim.

It is at this moment
A shot is fired.
The man falls through the snow
In a purity of fire –
Midnight
The fourth stroke of midnight.
The flame rivers his eyes
And the trees wither slowly
All over
Antrim.

Midnight
The fifth stroke of midnight –
A bomb
Explodes in the street
And a town dies.
The fire burning stones
A man searching for bones
A child counting the tears
Buried
In Antrim.

Now
We grow old.
The night springing with griefs
A fountain of flowers
At midnight
The sixth stroke of midnight
With snow falling
Through blood rising
Low down
For Antrim.

Midnight
The seventh stroke of midnight
The dead burying the dead
The earth moving the earth
Over the stilled mouths
Over the eyes
And the charred flesh
Whitening
Through Antrim.

Breathless
The air.
The soldiers ghosting through snow
Killing at shadows.
Midnight
The eighth stroke of midnight
A dream reaching for home
A bullet aimed at the stars
Echoes
Down Antrim.

Loss.
In just and unjust cause
We measure loss
At midnight
The ninth stroke of midnight.
Easing the ragged woes
Clutching the jagged ends
Watching the cold wars
Bleeding
White Antrim.

Midnight
The tenth stroke of midnight
The soldiers hunting for traps
The soldiers rooting through snow
The soldiers spilling with death
Black snow
Exploding
Now
Starlight
On Antrim.

Death.
At midnight
The eleventh stroke of midnight
Death –
In famine field and green beret
In the clothes we wore
At chapel, church and meeting
Death melting in snow
Still falling lightly –
My Antrim.

Midnight
The last stroke of midnight
Pounding
In Antrim.
Listen –
Midnight
Midnight
Midnight.
Exactly
Midnight.

Testament

Being
Of sound mind
I leave to Ireland
My remains.

The body
To be
Equally divided
Between the four provinces.

> *Found on the Antrim coast*
> *Two hands.*
> *No identifying marks.*

Being
Of unsound mind
I leave Ireland
To my body.

The four provinces
To be
Equally divided
Between my scattered remains.

> *Found near the city of Cork*
> *One torso.*
> *No identifying marks.*

2

Between
The graffiti and the idea
Lies the bomb.

Between
The idea and the explosion
Lies the cause

And this cause
We place
Under the protection

Of the most high God
Whose blessing we invoke
Upon our arms.

Found in the city of Dublin
One head.
No identifying marks.

3

Now
I do also bequeath
My two eyes

And therefore
My tongue and words
To those
Who would profit by them

And
I retain my seed
For loving
After death.

I do this
With malice aforethought
For in this wise
I do preserve my kind.

Sprawled on the rocks near Galway
One child –
Stillborn.

4

Autopsy Report:

I have examined these remains with special care and I have come
to the conclusion that the head, torso and hands are those of a middle-
aged man who lived in Ireland sometime during the nineteen seventies.
Cause of death – possibly an explosion. No way of knowing for sure
at this late date. Pity you couldn't have discovered the legs. I believe
the Irish were great runners in those days.

The child? Obviously a student prank. Refer this to the Anthropology Department.

5

Note found in a bottle
Washed up by the sea:
In this wise
I do preserve my kind.

Message to the Editor

Sir –

The Lord pardon the people of this town
Because I can't.
When I dropped dead in the street
Three weeks ago
I thought they'd bury me in style.
A state funeral was the least of it
With Heads of Government and the Nobility
In attendance.
I even looked forward to the funeral oration
In Irish
With a few words on my past achievements:
Our greatest poet, a seat in heaven to the man
And how I deserved better.

But did I get it?
My corpse lay in Baggot Street
For a fortnight
Before anyone noticed it.
And when I was finally removed
To the mortuary
I was abused by a medical student
Who couldn't open a bag of chips
Let alone the body of your greatest poet.
Then, to add to the indignity
I was pushed into an ice-box
And some clod stuck a label on my foot
Saying: unknown bard – probably foreign.

If it wasn't
For a drunken Corkman
Who thought I was his dead brother
I'd still be lying there unclaimed.
At least
The man had the decency to bury me.
But where am I?
Boxed in some common graveyard
Surrounded by peasants
And people of no background.
When I think of the poems I wrote
And the great prophecies I made
I could choke.

I can't write now
Because the coffin is too narrow
And there's no light.
I'm trying to send this
Through a medium
But you know what they're like –
Table-tapping bastards
Reeking of ectoplasm.
If you manage to receive this
I'd be glad if you'd print it.
There's no point in asking you
To send me a copy –
I don't even know my address.

The Wood Burners (1973)

The Wood Burners

Old women are made of wood
Blessed are the wood burners.

The unicorns of the night have come
And the silver priests and the nuns

We are the hunters of the dead
Holy holy in the bitter cold.

Black snow and bone crushed in the wind
The world is a ball of solid ice.

It is my thirteenth birthday
And no one writes to me.

My father is here and my stone mother
After us there will be nothing.

Christe! Christe!
Memento Mori.

She lies naked in the snow
Her arms broken and her head shaved

Flowers of blood circle her feet
And her tears anoint us

White nuns open her lips
And the priests possess her

My stone mother bathes her in oil
Under torches of snow.

Christe! Christe!
Memento Mori.

After us there will be nothing
We are the wood burners.

We drag her body to the hill
And watch it burn.

The fire eats her till noon
And then sleeps.

Only the bones remain
Damp wood under ashes of snow.

Memento Mori
I am me.

The seventh child in the last game
Iesu Christe.

Miss Cecily Finch

Miss Finch is dead.

In my day we lived south of the city
A large house, going cheap, and due for demolition.
In my day it was pleasant to live south of the city
And Miss Finch was forty years old.

Who was Miss Finch?
I wish I knew.

Her portrait hung upon the wall
In this house, going cheap, and due for demolition.
Her name printed underneath:
Miss Cecily Finch.
My house – bought and paid for in hard cash.

Miss Cecily Finch
Had money in the bank.

The house she lived in had a yellow face
The bathroom painted green
The stairs purple like a Roman Mass.
A country lass?
The dying roses in the hall proclaimed her taste.

Miss Cecily Finch
Had found her place.

When we moved in we cleaned the rooms
And swept the roses from the petalled hall
The stairs we painted white, the bathroom red,
Miss Finch was dead.
Her portrait, heavy on the nail, we dragged to the basement.

The door locked
On Miss Cecily Finch.

A famine week
And Dublin at its greyest peak
Shed tears of anguish for Miss Cecily Finch
Damp in the basement and crying to come out
I heard her shout: My house
Bought and paid for in hard cash.

Miss Cecily Finch
Ripe for demolition.

We set her free
Returned her portrait to the crumbling wall
Saw green grow on the bathroom shelf
And purple cover the stairs.
The dying roses in the street came back to greet
Miss Cecily Finch.

Who was Miss Cecily Finch –
A special case?
Her portrait hangs upon the wall
And dares me shift it from her chosen place.

The Madwoman of Cork

Today
Is the feast day of Saint Anne
Pray for me
I am the madwoman of Cork.

Yesterday
In Castle street
I saw two goblins at my feet
I saw a horse without a head
Carrying the dead
To the graveyard
Near Turner's Cross.

I am the madwoman of Cork
No one talks to me.

When I walk in the rain
The children throw stones at me
Old men persecute me
And women close their doors.
When I die
Believe me
They'll set me on fire.

I am the madwoman of Cork
I have no sense.

Sometimes
With an eagle in my brain
I can see a train
Crashing at the station
If I told people that
They'd choke me.
Then where would I be?

I am the madwoman of Cork
The people hate me.

When Canon Murphy died
I wept on his grave
That was twenty-five years ago.
When I saw him just now
In Dunbar Street
He had clay in his teeth
He blest me.

I am the madwoman of Cork
The clergy pity me.

I see death
In the branches of a tree
Birth in the feathers of a bird.
To see a child with one eye
Or a woman buried in ice
Is the worst thing
And cannot be imagined.

I am the madwoman of Cork
My mind fills me.

I should like to be young
To dress up in silk
And have nine children.
I'd like to have red lips
But I'm eighty years old.
I have nothing
But a small house with no windows.

I am the madwoman of Cork
Go away from me.

And if I die now
Don't touch me.
I want to sail in a long boat
From here to Roche's Point
And there I will anoint
The sea
With oil of alabaster.

I am the madwoman of Cork
And today
Is the feast day of Saint Anne.
Feed me.

The Leopard

Two lovers on a park bench
A leopard standing in the street.
It was a deep down and falling day
That will not come again.

The leopard lying in the street
Wondering how lovers meet
Heard:
Lover, when you came to me
I let you in
Knowing you had a husband.

Two lovers on a park bench
The leopard staring at the sun
Saw snow burning.

Sometimes
The leopard in his dream
Saw these two lying in his bed
Heard:
Touching your red red head
I curse the day you were wed.

Two lovers on a park bench
The leopard listening at the gate
Heard stars breaking.

Evening –
The leopard in his fire
Saw lips meet and apple breast
Heard:
Lover, I cannot bear the pain
Knowing we shall not meet again.

Two lovers on a park bench
The leopard crouching underneath.
It was a day gone and dying night.
The leopard sprang.

Birthday

Today
Being my fortieth birthday
My wife is here
And my two children
Maurice and Patrice.

The presents
Unwrapped upon the table
One from each
Are two seagulls made of glass
And a suit of mourning clothes.

It is three in the afternoon.
My wife kisses me on the cheek
My son leads me by the hand.
I must watch Patrice –
She comes to kill me.

David Gleeson

Poets of this country may now rejoice
Gleeson is dead!
Bailiff and bastard of the first order
Swimming in fire
May his greed choke him.

O Death! I forgive you all past iniquities
Now that you've swallowed him.
Gleeson the villain
The clod, the pox-faced twister
Who has plagued us for years.

Brazen, spiteful and crooked
His trade was cursed in every village
Jailing and persecuting poets
And other innocent people
He hounded us all.

Now he is dead
Burning and bleeding, jumping and roaring,
Captured in Hell.
The hand that plunged the dagger into his breast –
May it never grow less.

I shall die laughing.
The rending and gnashing of Gleeson's carcass
Which now hangs from the highest tree
Fills me with glee.
'Tis bloody fabulous!

(*Based on the Irish of Seán Ó Murchadha na Raithineach,
1700–62*)

Statement on the Burning of Cork

Yesterday
>Awoke with death

Heard church bells ring
>>Walked south to Cork.

Arriving there
>Sat for a while in silent prayer

A soldier strolling on the Mall
>>Smoked a slow pipe.

I saw that
>But I was not involved.

Continue.

Winter
>December the eleventh

Thought about snow
>And the coming Christmas.

Later
>With time to spare

Drank two whiskies
>In the 'Long Valley'.

I drank alone
>I spoke to no one

I am not gregarious.

Please continue.

Leaving there
>Moved north to shops

Bought several books
>Of a religious nature.

Six thirty
>In Albert Quay

Telephoned a friend
>Had personal contact.

Continue.

>The woman is a good friend
>Of excellent character
>And there is no question
>Of anything unseemly.

Please continue.

St Patrick's bridge was opened in 1895. It has three arches and is made of limestone. The old bridge was swept away in the great flood of 1853. Near the site of the old bridge there was a field known as Maggie's Dump. On the night of the flood, two brothers, having engaged each other in a fight, were both killed in this field. Some say, the brothers had taken different sides in a recent rebellion. Others say that they fought over a worthless woman. But where these two men fell no grass has ever grown. And the impression of their feet remains to this day.

Continue.

> I was not involved.

Please continue.

Ten thirty
> On the night in question

Passed by
> The Cork Opera House.

Saw this man
> On the front steps

Did not linger
> At this late hour.

The man's hair
> Was extremely long

I noticed this
> As I hurried on.

Continue.

Insanity is a disease of the mind. The Coal Quay is situated in Cornmarket Street. Many years ago, a person calling himself Jesus preached there. He said he was the son of God. He also said he was pregnant. On a certain night, this person hid himself in Katie Barry's rest-house and emerged several hours later carrying a female child. He claimed that this child was the Virgin Mary. He placed the child on the pavement, returned to Katie Barry's and shot himself. The child is now a ward of the Cork County Council and is reputed to be insane. The man who called himself Jesus is buried in St Finbarr's cemetery.

Oh, yes?

I am not involved.

Continue.

The man was naked
                From head to toe
I should have mentioned this
                Before.
He also stated
                I come in fear
To preach and pray
                In the city square.
Saw soldiers then
                Burning the city
Thought war, after all,
                Is a private matter.

Continue.

Three soldiers
                Of the British Crown
Marched past
                The Cork Opera House.
And this man
                In his condition
Denounced them
                And the British occupation.
Saw flames then
                Rising over Cork
And the City Hall
                Falling to the ground.
And these three
                Without contrition
Took this man
                And stoned him to death.

        I was not involved
        I am not involved
        I have no wish
        To be called as a witness.

Please sign.

The military barracks is closed to the public. The British soldier is never on view. Fifty years ago, a sentry was standing guard outside the armoury. It was midnight. The sentry looked at the door and was amazed to see a bear issuing from beneath it. He charged at the bear with his bayonet. The bayonet stuck in the door. The sentry fainted and was carried senseless to the guardroom. Two days later he was dead. And this story is entitled 'Ghosts and other curious phenomena'.

Loving

Leaning on a doorway of my mind
A singular death.

Georgette.

I had not seen her for a year
And then we met.
The bed we slept in
Was still warm from longing.

This in reply to questions
From two policemen:

How did she die?

From carbon monoxide poisoning.
I remember thinking – why?
And how many units of gas
To fill the lungs to bursting point.

She was good in bed
I said.

The first policeman stared at me
His friend studied the room
Covered the body of Georgette
Lit a cigarette.

How old was she?

Eighteen.
We thought as much.

She played pop music all night
The radio was on.
Those people upstairs
Thought you two were having a party.

I wasn't here.

Of course.
She left a note for you.

It's all here
How you promised to marry her.
Some people will never learn –
Are you married?

Yes.

Leaning on a doorway of my mind
A singular death.

Dispossessed

Pestilence has come to the land.
If I saw the men who caused it
Sitting at my table
I would eat them alive.

The trees in the orchard
Fall on my heart's grave.
The earth is a sea of bones
And nothing grows.

Only the rich can drink wine
And have full bellies.
They are the dregs who bartered all
And sent us into slavery.

It is a bitter thing
To be related to such vomit.
They murdered my wife
When she cursed their treachery.

Let them finish me too
I will not be silent.
My people lie on the roads
In a banquet of death.

And I will speak out
Wherever I go
Till the last breath
Is plundered from my body.

Lochan

When I die
Bury me in Sunday's Well
And on my grave
Place one red fuchsia tree.
Let me see the Lee
And hear strange talk
Of the Angels of Cork.

1

I am Lochan, son of Amirgin,
Great smith to MacHugh the Proud.
Here I subjugate myself
On this rock of many waters.

When I die
Coffin me in pure silver.

I am the seeker on these shores
It was I who burned the Great Marshes.
Lochan's coffin I stole from Gill Abbey Rock
His bones wrapped in pure silver.

When I die
Say for me a Mass of the Lances.

I am MacCarthy, Lord of Desmond,
Lately wed to a Norman wife
My blessing on the fair-haired Lochan
Whose wisdom was greater than my own.

When I die
Bury me alone.

I am the Phoenix of my race
Casting my dart beyond Munster waters
I ask Lochan for strength
To banish all hostile forces.

When I die
Cover me with wings of gold.

I am Warbeck, King of England,
Bound for Kent and Tyburn tree
I entreat the fair-haired Lochan
Heart and soul to comfort me.

When I die
Pity me.

I am Lochan, son of Amirgin,
Great smith to MacHugh the Proud.
Here I subjugate myself
Before God and Man.

2

I am O'Sullivan Beare
Eyries my dwelling place.
I ask of Jesus Christ
Through the intercession of Lochan
Damnation on all those
Who betrayed me for gold.

When my enemies attacked
My guns would not fire
My house was burned about my head
My servants were slaughtered.
Eternal fires torment those
Who hastened my destruction.

When I fell
They laid me out in the yard
For three days
For dogs to bite
For ravens to peck out my eyes.
The rain covered me.

Then on the fourth day
They roped my body to the keel
Of the King's sloop
And dragged me through the sea
From Berehaven to Cork.
There, they beheaded me.

They spiked my skull
On the wall of the South Gate prison
Cast my body in the sewers
For rats to chew –
O'Sullivan Beare
Champion of my people.

Now I ask Jesus Christ to raise me up
I ask Lochan to restore my dwelling place
To guard my people in time of need
To bless them with arms.
Let no man house my enemies –
They must be boned and ragged.

I am O'Sullivan Beare.

3

I am Lochan, son of Amirgin,
Great smith to MacHugh the Proud.
Here I renounce all darkness
And send forth arrows of light.

When I rise
Follow me with new beginnings.

I am Shannon of this Parish
Long dead with high famine
My flesh blows from the ridge
Near Goul-na-Spurra.

When I rise
I will devour my bones.

I am Aideen without blessing
Since I tasted my own child
Should I live to see the morrow
Christ blind me and conceal my mouth.

When I rise
Desiccate my womb.

I am Lochan, son of Amirgin,
Great smith to MacHugh the Proud
On this rock I shed blood tears
Mourning my people through a black starvation.

When I rise
Cover me with bleeding.

4

Where have they gone
My chosen people?
I am beseeched by shadows.

The Lord MacCarthy is no more
The banquet halls are empty
His soldiers vanquished.

Where is O'Sullivan Beare?

His land is a heap of stones
His rooms desolate.
Who will deliver us?

From the Red Abbey tower
I search the skies
For a winged Redeemer.

The clouds are bones
The gulls screech
In a firmament of fire.

Where is Lochan?

His children gnaw at the earth
In a fever of jaws.
The crows mock them.

Only the sea remains
Washing the dead.
I am Cormac

Beseeched by shadows.

5

I am Lochan, son of Amirgin,
Great smith to MacHugh the Proud.
From Gill Abbey Rock I have seen my angels
Rise in splendour from the Great Marsh.

I am Bridget of these rivers:
The Lee, the Bandon, and Blackwater.
I beheld the fair-haired Lochan
Walk in fire through Gill Abbey Rock.

I am Finbarr, saint of Munster.
Where I stand
Sanctify my eagles.

Christ in London (1960)

Song for a Poor Boy

When he was young he had no sense
And souls were sold for eighteen pence
While he ran mad in streets of gold
And people said he must be old
And hard as nails.

When hunger tore the windows out
And all the rooms were steeped in sin
He prayed to witches in his bed
And painted all the doorknobs red
And danced and sang.

But sticks and stones came tumbling down
When he put on his royal gown
And overright the convent wall
We dressed him in his mother's shawl
And broke his back.

And strong men went to take his soul
When he refused his begging bowl
But he was made to stretch his wings
And lead a company of kings
And touch the stars.

And silver ghosts leapt from his hand
When famine raged across the land
We locked him in a padded cell
And said he'd surely go to hell
And twist and burn.

But in the dark he learned to creep
When all the guards were fast asleep
And in his house of spinning pearls
We hopped about in loops and whirls
And rang the bell.

We chained him to the madhouse floor
And heard his long night goblin's roar
He split the chain and smashed the lock
And stopped the white wall ticking clock
And climbed the stair.

We held him down inside his tomb
We robbed his heart and fired his room
He watched us from his bony place
And all the seas ran down his face
And drained the world.

But when the lamps were going down
He made himself a one-eyed clown
He saw the sun fall through the skies
And knew that all we knew was lies –
And grinned and grinned.

from Roxy's

Prologue

Night
And the leaves of snow
Night and the blinding quays
A child crying in the Marsh
And the Shandon ringing.

The river is a road of ice
The people wither in their beds
And only stone birds speak
When Kings are out
In the cruel night
And the starving snow.

Coats up and mind your face
Christ was a fool to save mankind
The Devil is a snowman in a race
And ice is Hell.
Here in the city there's a place
For all his men.

Robed in the burning white
The Guards are an arrow in the snow
And Queens at the Connie gate
Wear blood for boots
Red in the long bright
And the sounding world.

Saunters grinning in her hair
The night is a candle to her bed
The pennies jingle on the stair
And mouths are moons.
Locked in the city and the fair
The bones break out.

Night
And the ghost of Hell
Night and the frozen bell
Black in Sunday's Well
And a light in Roxy's.

1 Roxy's

All down from the iron hills
All down from the Windy Gap
The silver lights are going out
And the green ice cracks.

The old men rise from drunken beds
The young men creep from village holes
All down to a starving town
All down to Roxy's.

Now raise your glass
And drink, my love
The ice is breaking through the floor
We'll take the virgin from your brow
And hang your kisses on the door.

The frost is black
Your face is white
The world is falling through your hair
O raise your glass and still, my Dove
We'll ride the whirlwind of love.

We'll sit in circles round the lamp
We'll drink our whiskey from a jar
When Queens fly out to sing and dance
In long black shawls.

And, Holy Father, watch us pray
The light of Heaven shine on us
And close the window and the door
And bleed the night.

All down at the falling sky
All down at the burning end
Being your kettle and your drum
Seven days to Kingdom Come.

2 First Confession

Holy Father, I killed a cat!
And what the devil were you playing at?
A thing like that
Killing a cat!

Holy Father, it happened today
As I was going upon my way
To buzz a drum and make a play
For the bird in the upstairs room.
I met this gish one windy night
And, Holy God, she was a sight!
The finest gams you ever saw
And tits like the blaze of noon.

I tracked her out along Park Lane
Her backside swinging in the rain
And, Father, I was in desperate pain
At the thought of her old Ding Dong.
I tried, God knows, to say a prayer
But I was stuffed to the gills in beer
I danced in the lane as she went in
And whistled the Raper's Song.

And then last night I passed her place
And thought to myself what a drum to case
I'll get me gear and change me face
Dive in creep out and gone.
And then I thought, sure what the Hell!
I'll grab the bird and ride the swell
There's no point slinging her down a well
Till I've fiddled her old Ding Dong!

And, Father, I rose at half past five
When tarts are dead or half alive
But as I saddled from me dive
I came across that cat.
His coat coal black and eyes blood red
I should have stayed at home in bed
But, Father, I bashed him over the head
And laid him out on the mat!

My son, my son, what have you done?
There's no absolution for that!
And God in his mercy will tear you alive
For raising your maw to a cat.

4 Lackery

Two eyes bald and sunken in
Curses where his heart had been
Murder running down his face
Chasing Christ about the place
Angels dancing down and out
Demons swimming in his mouth.
A holy light swept from his head
He damned the Kings and wished us dead.

At turn of night we heard him roar
And burn the world on every whore
He lashed them all and rang the bell
For every flame that circled Hell.
He saw the stars and mountains meet
And flood and famine round his feet.
He raised his hand and turned his face
To blast and scald the human race.

We killed the light in every room
We painted out the listening moon
A knife was rivered down his spine
His head we buried deep in wine
And all around we heard his breath
Give out the drunken sound of death.
We washed his soul in fire and scrump
And lugged him out to Galley's Dump.

5 Remember the Night?

HE: You remember the night
We stood in the hall
And the rain coming down
And your father upstairs in the loft
Reciting the Rosary?
Well that was the night
I walked home in a flood
And woke up the next morning in bed
With double pneumonia.

SHE: Well it might have been that
Or it might have been caused by a draught
Or the strain on your legs
As you stood in the door
With your trousers half down
One hand on the latch
And the other on me
And an ear cocked upstairs
For my father reciting the Rosary

HE: You remember the night
We sat on the step
And I mentioned to you
That you weighed half a ton at the least
In spite of your looks?
Well that was the night
Going home in the dark I fell into a ditch
And woke up the next morning in splints
And several fractures.

SHE: Well it might have been that
Or it might have been lust
And all them cortortions and fits
You got up to in spite of the frost
And the narrow old step
And the fact that the whole bloody thing
Was completely insane
When you think I was wearing a shawl
And a long pair of labourer's trousers.

HE: You remember the night
    I stayed in your room
    And your father lepped out of his bed
    And came down in a rage
    And dropped dead on the spot?
    Well that was the night
    I passed out with the shock
    And I couldn't make out why he died
    Do you think it was age?

SHE: Well it might have been that
     Or it might have been seeing you there
     With your shirt on the floor
     Your fingers caught up in the springs
     You roaring with laughter
     My dress on the wall
     A gin bottle under the bed
     And his rosary missing for weeks
     Slung under the mat.

· HE: Well, yes – it might have been that.

6 The Stag

Brothers! lock and bar that door
And drag that scorpion to the floor.
His tongue in every Garda's ear
With every word we spoke in here.
We'll drag his tongue out by the roots
And dance on him with iron boots
We'll split his lip and take his hand
In frost and fire throughout the land.

Tonight a brother walks his cell
Tomorrow screaming down to Hell.
The crows will rip his nose and mouth
The worms will wander in and out
While you lie here as free as sin
Guzzling biddy scrump and gin.
The Cross of Christ will melt your name
And every stag who plays the game.

The candles blazed and cut the night
We slit his throat and bled him white
The Devil rot his kith and kin
He'll never speak the word again.
We broke his back and smashed his face
And scattered him about the place.
Now when they come to find their prize
They'll see the hounds jump through his eyes.

7 The Kings are Out

In Patrick Street
In Grattan Street
In Ireland Rising Liberty Street
The Kings are out.

Along the Mall
The Union Quay
In every street along the Lee
The Kings are out.

With knives of ice
And dressed to kill
The wine flows down from Summer Hill
Christ! Be on your guard tonight
The Kings are out.

The snow is dark
And where they meet
The blood in rivers at their feet
Christ! be on your guard tonight
The Kings are out.

Armies marching through the snow
Banners burning row on row
Hate upon them as they go
The stars are red.

Parnell Bridge is falling down
South Gate Bridge is falling down
The City Hall is falling down
The stars are red.

Christ! Be on your guard tonight
The Kings are out.

2

Walking through the fire and flame
Holy Father racked in pain
Corpus Christi in his hand
  Make way for the Lord!

Murder, rape, and sudden death
Got your bloody onions yet?
Pay the birds and never fret
   Go home to God!

Gaze upon this dreadful sight
Send an arrow through the night
Crush them to a bolt of Hell
   Make way for the Lord!

Holy Father, mind your ways
You belong to other days
Now the Kings write all the plays
   Go home to God!

Down the Mall he walks in prayer
Buildings burning everywhere
Pushing Christ before the world
   Make way for the Lord!

And the Kings with bone and knives
Tear away his hundred lives
Throw his body in the Lee
   Go home to God!

3

Kings and Queens march on the town
Someone wears a royal crown.

And the old ones in the street
Ring the dead bell of defeat.

Reason bleeding through the snow
Nowhere else on Earth to go.

Mother of God be our relief
Close the world on all our grief.

4

Dance to a royal tune
Down to a darkening moon
Under the rivers of frost
Cry the believers.

Deep in the silver ground
Damned in the fire and sound
Under the billows of ice
Cry the believers.

5

And the churches collapsed
And they opened the graves
And they moved in a wind
Through a fever of dead
And a babble of bones.
They raged at the lock
And they tore down the walls
And they danced on the pillars of blood
And the arches of gold.

They burned at the Rock
And they staggered the root
And they struck at the wound
And the cry in the dark cathedrals.
They gouged out the eyes
And they murdered the lips
And they buried the tongue
And the voice in the vile eclipses.

And the city destroyed
And they ravaged the light
And they rode on a storm
Through an ocean of grief
And a terror of ice.
They stretched on the shores
And they raved at the stars
And they cursed at the roof of the world
And the finger of God.

6

Death by the skulls of night
Dark by the fearful blight
Under the falling skies
Cry the believers.

Dead on the bitter glow
Dust on the burning snow
Under the galleys of Hell
Cry the believers.

7

In Patrick Street
In Grattan Street
The Kings are out.

The gallows high
Across the sky
The Kings are out.

Along the Mall
The Union Quay
In every street along the Lee
Eternal night
The cinders white
The Kings are out.

The starving world
Has turned to stone
The Kings are out.

The Queens alone
Lie bone to bone
The Kings are out.

And through the green and bitter hate
The cry of eagles at the gate:
CHRIST BE ON YOUR GUARD
    TONIGHT
THE KINGS ARE OUT.

Christ in London

Tonight
With London's ghost
I walk the streets
As easy as November fog
Among the reeds.
Along the Strand
I heard the lovers say:
Look out for love
And keep the wolves at bay.

Tonight
The white birds
Settle on the moon
The roads are black
The buildings flash and burn.
At Tyburn tree
I heard the hangman say:
Look out for death
And keep the crowds away.

Tonight
The mist lies cold
On London's face
The walls are grief
The souring trees grow tall
And in Whitehall
I heard the Guardsman say:
Look out for war
And keep the guns for play.

The guns for play
The crowds away
The wolves at bay
And London's ghost cried out:
Look hard on me.
In every street
I heard his dead voice say:
The skies are green
And all my loves are clay.

2

Is that you there?
I'll lead you down the hall
The drunken soldier's gone
Now mind, don't fall.
Christ! But the girls are stiff
Against the wall
The City Road's a curse
And few will call.

Take off your coat
I'll strip and draw the blind
You're safe and sound in here
My heart you'll find
Robed in a deepdown love
And I'll be kind
And dress the wounds
That reef a young man's mind.

O but he comes to steal
To rend and tear
He drives the arrow deep
And binds my hair.
With thorns of grinning ice
And sick despair
He drags my soul for love
And calls me fair.

My love, my life, my hope
My losing bride
Tonight the world is lost
And blowing wide
And now with London's ghost
I've killed my pride
And all my tears run down
Your grieving side.

Yes, that's the way
Good-night and mind your prayers
Look out for love
And girls who hunt in pairs.
The Big Ben clock strikes one
And down the stairs:
Good-night, my love
And joy drive out your fears.

3

Drive out my fears tonight
From Burning Wood
For here I stand in chains
With London's ghost.
The Big Ben clock strikes two
And Christ is born
With tongues of rust and fire
And arms of gold.

The leaves are red with blood
The roots are burned
The flowering stones are knives
Beneath the trees
The Naked Man runs wild
Through London's streets
And terror rakes the night
Above the town.

The hungry Cross stands guard
Inside the wood
The Roman legions march
Across the tomb
The eagle bends and breaks
The iron mask
And Christ walks out to greet
The starving bones.

I see your face
And murder on your brow
When nettles spring with steel
And mountains bleed.
I see your sorrows
Stretched across the stars
And feel your limbs pressed cold
Against the moon.

4

From Burning Wood
I walked with London's ghost
The Big Ben clock struck three
Across the Thames
In Notting Hill
I heard the White Man say:
Tonight the Blacks go down
We'll carve them good!

The boughs will crack
The rocks will spin and fall
Tonight the Blacks are pinned
Against the wall
And we'll come down in blood
Upon them all
With hooks and spears and knives
We'll carve them good!

We'll drive the bugs in spades
From Notting Hill
The jungle patch will be
Their grinding mill
For here in town
We've had our bloody fill
We'll cut them down in style
We'll carve them good!

And let the Law come out
And stand and stare
We're all tooled up tonight
The wind is fair.
We'll drag the bastards screaming
Through the Square
With hooks and spears and knives
We'll carve them good!

Tonight we'll skin the breed
We'll spread the crop
We'll burn the Blackies white
Before we stop
And you can laugh to see
Them skip and hop
We'll rip them up in rags
We'll carve them good!

Look out for death
And daggers down your spine
The Big Ben clock strikes four
Across the Thames
In Notting Hill
I heard the White Man say:
With hooks and spears and knives
We carved them good.

5

And still with London's ghost
I crossed the town
The Big Ben clock struck five
And Christ was old.
The Roman soldier killed
The golden fox
And hid the bones
Inside the robber's tomb.

And no one saw
The sleeping cockerel turn
From dream of doves
To hammer, flint and nails
And no one saw
The lonely horseman bleed
When furies blazed and curled
Inside the rose.

The London crowds rode out
With grins and jeers
They wore their Sunday coats
Their flashing shoes
And Christ fell through the wounds
And split the world
With frost and fire and bone
And crown of thorns.

They buried him
Beneath the London streets
The concrete in his mouth
His heart in flames
The Roman soldier played
His game of cards
And watched the sky for blood
And wings of war.

6

Bring out the drums
And roll the willing slave
The Big Ben clock strikes six
And fools are brave.
In Oxford Street
They've built an open grave
Where mouths will rot
And banners rant and rave.

The coloured lamps go down
And all is said
When teeth and fingers claw
The human head
The longboned soldier rapes
The bridal bed
And drives the broken lance
Through London's dead.

Look out for war
And cinders in your eyes
The howling dogs have met
The dark gulls rise
And here with London's ghost
I see the prize
And hear his voice break out
Across the skies:

Oh Christ! the day will come
And men will hide
The Thames will split its banks
The seas divide
A sword will cross the sun
And Hell break wide
And I shall crush the lamb
And drown the bride.

The Universe will shake
And flesh will flower
And I will make of souls
A human tower.
The stars will vomit blood
And hour by hour
The beaks and claws will snap
And jaws devour.

7

At dawn
With London's ghost
I walked the streets
And black as coal
I scratched among the ruins.
Beneath the walls
I heard the lovers say:
Look out for love
And keep the wolves at bay.

At dawn
The blue dust
Blows across the town
The lips are laced with blood
The eyes are holes
Inside the tomb
I heard the hangman say:
Look out for death
And keep the crowds away.

At dawn
The briars grow wild
On London's face
The fingers twist and crawl
Inside the dove
And to his love
I heard the Guardsman say:
Look out for war
And keep the guns for play.

The guns for play
The crowds away
The wolves at bay
And London's ghost cried out:
Look hard on me.
Upon these rocks
We both sat down to pray
Till Christ rose up
And struck the Rising Day.

Heart of Grace (1959)

My Little Red Knife

With my little red knife
I met my love
With my little red knife
I courted
And she stole me to her deep down bed
Her hair spread out a burning red
But never a single word was said
About my little red knife.

With my little red knife
I held her down
With my little red knife
I kissed her
And there in the deep of her two blue eyes
I kissed and kissed a thousand lies
And opened wide her golden thighs
To please my little red knife.

With my little red knife
I made her weep
With my little red knife
I loved her
And the wine was heavy in her mouth
The morning air stood up to shout
But there wasn't a living soul about
To see my little red knife.

With my little red knife
I raised her up
With my little red knife
I ripped her
And there in the gloom and rolling night
I cut her throat by candlelight
And hurried home to my waiting wife
Who damned my little red knife.

An Caisideach Bán

The grass will not grow on the side of the hill
And the moon will make no light at all
Great is the sorrow of love to my mind.
Death stands beside me laughing.

There is trouble upon my soul
There is bitterness all about me
My heart is a hard black coal
Since that woman left me alone.

She was the daughter of a steward
With kine and oceans of gold
Not of my station at all –
That is a bitter love.

At the head of the steep stairs
Is the woman of the white breasts
But she is not my love
Though we have spoken many times.

I would build her a house of leaves
I would build her a house of gold
Were you to offer me the Great Harvest
I would not give you her amber hair.

The meaning of life has died
Let the fish swim without water
Let the white waves destroy great mountains
But I cannot betray her.

English was not my speech
But I learned it to please my girl
But I was a fool without sense
Like a small bird on a tall tree.

Once I went to college
And I reached the time of my tonsure
Five years I spent in a school
But my love tore it from me.

My fear of God is grief
Maybe there is no mercy
My sin is beyond all measure
Because of the love I gave her.

Coming toward me like a swan
Beautiful as your own love.
Pity she was born of her mother's womb
To be my cold death.

She sits on the far hill
Playing music day and night.
Christ, though she has brought me to this
Preserve her from all harm.

The White Monument

Look you: Do not despise him
For you are strangers here and do not know
You do not know how beautiful he was
How great was his battle-power
You come with your new books
And little silver pencils
But you do not know how tall he was.

Now he is dead!
The Great Bull of the city is dead.
The Civic Guards come down from Barrack Street
With iodine on their lips
And black ink on their fingers.
They stand like old warriors
Before the white monument.

The crowd gathers in the Mall
And the little girls tremble.
The Trinity bell breaks out
And then there is silence.
Even the boys have stopped singing
For no one can believe
The Great Bull is dead.

The seagulls come up the river
And settle on the monument
The old men at the Fountain
Fold their papers and whisper
Of the rich blood of the Bull.
Now the dockers come up from the Quay
To gaze at the beautiful body

Lying on the Mall
There with the green sword in his mouth
On that black tar since night
In the crying whirlpool of blood
Since soft terrible night –
Look you: It was the Earth breaking
And the stars falling on us.

All the Civic Guards are wondering
All the people are wondering
Many of them have fierce looks.
The pencils cut through the black books
And the seagulls watch from the monument
Wondering who stabbed
Wondering who dared with a green sword.

Who killed him cried the monument?
Who cut him cried the stone figures?
Who dragged at the long wound
Opened the soft mouth
To anoint
To embalm with sour death?
And the old men at the Fountain
Dropped their papers and wept.

The tall girls trembled
The women brought heaps of flowers
Garlands of burning nettles
To lay at the feet at the bright head
To cover the pouring wound
To seal the starved eyes
Of the murdered Bull.

Who stabbed the Great Bull in the mouth?
Who killed the Great Pride?
If not names then reasons
We are all wondering
We don't know
It is time we did know
Who rose in the cruel night and killed.

Now all the bells rang
And the Shandon timed the ringing
The dockers pulled down the flags
And covered the face of the Bull
The seagulls rested on the body
The children tugged at the green sword
And broke the long blade to pieces.

The Naked Man was torn and bled
And he walked over the body of the Bull
Whispering: who killed killed the Great Power?
The Civic Guards looked at the stone figures
And the white monument cursed.
Who killed killed the Great Power?
And the blood flashed in the sunlight.

Ah! Here was a death.
The great death, the cruel death.
The proud Bull of the city upon the Mall
Covered with flags and flowers
And burning burning nettles.
And no one knows who killed him –
O we are wondering.

*   *   *

In the evening we buried him
We raised him on our shoulders
And walked with him to Douglas.
All the windows draped in seaweed
And the streets filled with iron ghosts
The blood grew hard upon the road
And we buried him.

We crossed the bridges and the Quays
And the children carried flowers
We passed the Deadhouse and the Union Gate
And the people wept for him.
The Civic Guards wore black hats
And the soldiers wore suits of green.
There under a tall tree we buried him.

You do not know how we felt
It is too great to imagine,
But there was never such a death as this
Never such a lament.
It was the blood shooting from the wounds
A cistern of fires.
It was the most killing of all deaths
And we could not believe it.

The Civic Guards marched past
And they would not believe it
The wound was plain to see
But we would not see it.
We covered his face with earth and ferns
And saw that the blood was gone.
Still we would not believe it.

When the voice of God told us
We did not listen.
When the red wind shrieked at us
We did not hear it.
We dragged his body from the grave
And saw how he was dead –
But we did not believe in death.

Then when it was over we asked ourselves:
Who would do such a thing?
Who would take the Great Pride
And murder him with a sword?
We questioned the Civic Guards and the soldiers
And we questioned ourselves,
But no one knew who killed us with a death.

*   *   *

Now upon this old night
We knelt upon a rock of leaves
And stared before us to the hungry hills.
The coloured lamps upon the wall
Threw daggers at the face of God
Melting the little caves of ice
From his two eyes.

Was it ourselves alone
Who broke the night with moving
Was it ourselves alone
Who silenced the stone figures
Was it ourselves alone
Destroyed the outraged centuries
Killing the Great Pride with our consent?

The weeds grow over the Great Bull
And children walk the Douglas Road.
The Naked Man whispers to the night:
It was ourselves alone
Who stabbed him with a green sword
Stabbed him in the mouth in the night

And we did not know?

Madasha

Young Madasha grew afraid of the Twilight creeping
Slowly creeping over and over the Twilight Isle
And young Madasha knelt down and prayed
And young Madasha prayed aloud
To the madhouse Gods of the daylight sleeping
For strength to kill the Twilight creeping
Over and over the Twilight Isle.

And the madhouse Gods came down from the tree
Down from the tree to Madasha's side
And they promised Madasha the strength of a bull
A hundred horses and a hundred men
But first, Madasha must sell his soul
And sell his eyes to a raving king
And Madasha must find the Royal Blackbird
That left Glencree on a broken wing.

And Madasha swore he would sell his soul
For the strength of a hundred thousand bulls,
He would sell his eyes to any old king
For a thousand horses and a thousand men.
The Gods now told him to kill the moon
And Madasha promised to do it soon
As he watched the Twilight slowly creeping
Over and over the Twilight Isle.

Madasha flew to the cave of the moon
And he watched her bathe in the eye of noon,
He broke her back with a heavy tree
Dragged her down to the splattering sea;
He kissed her cheek as he pushed her in
And flooded the valley with all his tears.
The eagle watching from Ireland's nest
Broke his heart in his iron breast.

And as he cried, the Twilight moved
Slowly creeping over and over
And the madhouse Gods gave Madasha strength
Till his hands grew larger than all the Earth,
Larger than Heaven and Hell itself;
And he beat the Twilight with golden bars
And the sparks that flew made countless stars –
But still the Twilight moved.

Then Madasha paused to gain more strength
While Twilight grew on the Emigrant style
And slowly it moved again and again
Slowly reeling over the land.
Then Madasha roared till the Earth grew deaf
And the World's axis split in two
And Madasha stood in the empty void
Pushing the Twilight with hands of fire.

He pushed it back to the daylight sea
Where the waves were lions and horses' hooves,
And Madasha pushed it under the sea
While the lions danced and the hooves thundered
Till the Twilight hit the deepdown rocks
And died as the waves grew small
All for Madasha
Who waited to wash his hands and face.

Then Madasha sang to the madhouse Gods
The king returned Madasha's eyes
And the Devil leapt out through Hell's green gate
With Madasha's soul on a silver plate.
And slowly Madasha's hands grew small,
He built for his people a golden hall
And he smiled as he watched the sunlight growing
Over and over the Sunlight Isle.

A Day of Rebellion

Softly
As if the world might break with moving
This little army rested on the city.
Rifles and green jackets
Bullets for empty pockets
Careful of the British soldier
Standing sentry against the sun.

And so we took the tram from Donnybrook
And wondered if we had to pay
For this was Revolution Day
When all the soldiers play:
This is the nation of the free,
Drown all the others in the sea.

And at high noon
The eagles of this ancient race
Gathered together on High Rock.
The blood groaned heavy on the pavements
The windows opened and the rifles cracked
Fire and gold rode through the streets

For Liberty, Equality and Death.

And we maintain
The right of the Irish people
To the unfettered control . . .

Of Liberty, Equality and Death.

All but the beating of wings!
Think of the death it brings
The bodies falling from the roof
And then where's the proof?
The nettles growing in Parnell's mouth
The blood raining from the stars.

O'Leary's ghost in Sackville Street
Where all young heroes meet
Fionn and Cúchulain of the Ford
Pearse with his pamphlet of the free –
They died for liberty
Sagart Aroon.

Don't let this Easter pass
All the gentry trotting off to Mass
Snipers lying on the roof
On the Four Courts, on Boland's Mill
This day we'll drink our fill
Of Liberty, Equality and Death.

And we place this cause
Under the protection of the most high God
Whose blessing we invoke
Upon our arms
And we pray
Never to relent
Signed on behalf of the Provisional Government.

O Leinster's wound is wide
With every shot that sings
Over the swollen river.
The blood is hard upon the walls
And no one shall deface
The glory of this ancient race.

O Leinster's wound is blowing wide
And April cuts the root.

*   *   *

Sweet young girl from Evergreen
Dressed to kill in Irish green
Finest girl ever seen
Dead with a bullet through her head
Stone dead with a bullet through her head
Round and round we go . . .

And Logan standing on the bridge
Dreamed an evening with Maloney's mott
While Maloney played soldiers in the street
To the tramp tramp of marching feet
Till he was shot dead
With a bullet through the head.

And she with a boxcar full of loot
Sang 'Down with the English and the Jews
Three cheers for the Rebels and the Blues'
(O the right of the people to wear shoes!)
Till a bullet from a German gun
Stopped her dead.

Christ! Me heart's blood is pouring away
Like a great river
Me new shawl is drenched with blood
And some bastard has pinched me purse –
O no one gives a tinker's curse
For Maloney's mott

Stone dead
With a bullet through her head.

An English pound wrapped round her yellow garter
(Go on, Mick! I know what you're after)
Katie played the fiddle in a Dublin snug
Wept for the English and the Irish dead
Drowned her sorrows in a jar of stout –
Business should pick up before the night is out

But she was dead
With a bullet through her head.
Smashing windows, blinding glass,
A bullet through the open door
And now the fiddle on the sawdust floor
Playing music no more.

All dead
With a bullet through the head
Stone dead.

Liberty, Equality and Death.

*   *   *

Softly
As if the world might break with moving
They walked over the bodies of the dead
The flag is burning on the GPO
Now tell me where all good Christians go?
Christ with his side pierced through
Is terrified of English cannon.

All for a twilight of history!
The red horses rearing at the sun
The children playing among the lilies
Dry skulls turning in the dust
Where are the preachers and the just?
My Johnny has gone for a soldier
Och anee!

Burning buildings
Pavements cracked
Yellow frost
And windows smashed

Women screaming
Green and red
Children thieving
Loaves of bread

Iron guards
With skulls of brass
Fingers filled
With a fountain of knives.

*   *   *

And nowhere
Have our lines been broken through
An Ireland glorious and new
Worthy of her place
Heroes of this noble race . . .

Who looked at Connolly's face?

The eagles whispered on High Rock
The arrows pierced Cuchulain's feet
The Irish rebel with his sword of glass
Swore he would never go to Mass:
Put all the clergy in their place!

Who looked at Connolly's face?

Old news to the generations
Riding through the green sky
Wearing their glittering swords
Sounding their hollow trumpets
Till the heavens burst open
And it was blight of day.

Old news
Dead and buried deep.

*   *   *

And Pearse was demented
No denying that!
Standing there with his pamphlet
And his cocked hat
What do you think of that?

And who were they all
I'd like to know?
Freedom in the GPO
That lot will have to go!
Death.

And as for the rest
Who cares
Twopence a pound the apples and pears
Wait till I get you upstairs
Stopping out all night.

Round and round we go.

*   *   *

When Albion's demon rolled the tide
Slinging her blazing irons at the stars
There was death.

Lying over the broken rifles
Over the bugles
Nailed to the stakes of history
A bellowing rage of agony

The Earth heaves
The prisoners are dead
The rain falls eternally
And down
Over this sickening fuchsia.

Who'll sing 'Sixteen Dead Men'
Never to rise again
In the Western World?

Softly – lightly
As if the world might break with moving
We scrawled their names upon the glass
And saw forever
Through the burning world.

Chicken Coop

Once upon a time and a good time coming
It was too, they told me the story.
But why tell me when I alone know the fluffy yarn.
Never upon any time but the time they made
Came down upon us all, not once but twice or more.
Let me tell tale of Chicken Coop.

When the cock of the ultra barmy world
Fell over a matchbox and picked up a mad sixpence
And shot all opposing ducks with brain-water,
The quiet unmanageable hens of the feathered house
Chopped off his head and watched it squiggle and squirt
In the victorian silence that ruled the modern mansion.

This, without any doubt of shape or cold fancy
Was a minor upheaval in the clucking coop.
To see the white silk blood of the cock was one thing
But to be confronted with four fat hens
Spreading sour butter on blackrationed bread
And gulping jars of pink jam like angels was another!

There would have to be a sane-holy discussion,
A meeting or something to settle the half matter.
There sat the chief hen, fat and chewing a smoke-leaf
Pretending he did not agree knowing that he did.
All the other hens clucked and mucked about
Telling each other the opposite to what they thought.

Should there or should there not be an objection
To the progressive use of paying pennies to oblige nature?
Should male hens be allowed to visit female ducks
In the bawdiness of their boudoir after midnight?
No agreement was reached on this sensitive point
And they clucked clacked clucked till the small hours.

Then to the surprise of no one at all
They murdered each other with kindness,
Wore pink multi-coloured underwear to celebrate
And danced over the dead breathing body of the cock.
To have a hooley was one thing
But to have a skip-jap scamping dance in misery was not!

Four pots of jellied jam were ordered
Along with a contingent of nuts, guns
Bombs or green eggs, several thick slices of propaganda
To conceal the not quite so obvious intent
Of the feathered smoking one and the McGrath whippet
That sat sulking and mulking in the half hole.

All the other hens were plucked to the white bone
And now fluttered about naked and covering their places
To keep the cold thoughts away from their eyes.
Lemon – bitter and tasteless – was eaten or devoured
And amid the clocking and mocking of the far-seeing naïve
They danced themselves to death and mother glory.

Now there is nothing in the Chicken Coop
Save perhaps a bucket or two of crimson soup
That the few invading peacocks washed their tails in.
Feathers paint the walls in gaudy colours
And the drunken Hamlet of his distant calling father
Sits pondering on the use of reason: reason is the question.

Notes

Only the Mad

'The mad could be the artist, the outsider, or "The Naked Man".' (From a series of interviews with Galvin, conducted by Greg Delanty, June–September 1995. All further references, *Interviews*.) See also 'Christ in London', p. 101; and 'The White Monument', p. 114.

For One Who Disappeared

Written for a Chilean friend of Galvin's who visited him when he lived in Belfast. She had never seen snow. After returning to Chile, where she was arrested and held as a political prisoner, she disappeared.

The Oldest Man in Gernika

Gernika, Basque spelling of Guernica. 'The first city to be blitzed by German aircraft during the Spanish Civil War. A local artist who signed himself "García" drew a picture of the oldest tree in Gernika, where the first democratic parliament is reported to have taken place. There are railings round this tree now. People throw coins over the railings.' (*Interviews*). Pablo Picasso painted a famous picture of the city's destruction, referred to in part 4.

The Wall

Written while Galvin lived in Ballycotton, Co. Cork. See biography.

Plaisir d'Amour

'. . . partially fiction, partially true about my parents, true to my parents' inner lives and relationship. My father disappeared in his mind to India where he had spent time as a British soldier in the Royal Munster Fusiliers during the First World War. He often talked about washing himself in the Ganges and bragged that he was the only man in Cork to have done so. He loved India.' (*Interviews*).

'ghett': Hiberno-English for a bastard, or brat. Also survives in Scots.

The Wood Burners

'Based on the last burning of witches in Ireland, in 1895, and the attitude to women, especially the religious attitude that women had no souls.' (*Interviews*). Bridget Cleary was burned to death in Ballyvaden, a village near Clonmel, on 15 March 1895. Galvin based his play, *The Last Burning* (1974) on that event.

'Memento Mori': Latin, 'Remember that you have to die.'

The Madwoman of Cork

'the feast day of Saint Anne': 26 July. St Anne was the mother of the Virgin Mary.

David Gleeson

Based on the Irish of Seán Ó Murchadha na Ráithíneach (1700–32), poet and scribe from Carrignavar, near Cork, who supported the Jacobite cause and rebellion against the English authorities.

Statement on the Burning of Cork

This poem is in the form of a reluctant statement by an observer of the burning of Cork on 11 December 1920, when the Black and Tans (non-Irish personnel drafted into the Royal Irish Constabulary to combat the IRA campaign of 1920–21) went on a rampage through the city in reprisal for an ambush carried out on them. 'It is written out of Cork history and also its folklore . . . The man who called himself Jesus . . . went around with a pillow under his jersey . . . He thought he was Jesus, but was about to give birth to the Virgin Mary.' (*Interviews*).

'Katie Barry's': A famous Cork shebeen or illegal drinking place of dubious reputation near the Coal Quay.

Lochan

'Lochan': Given name of St Finbarr, patron saint of Cork, where his cult flourished although he is unlikely to have visited there.

'Amirgin': Legendary and archetypal Irish poet who came with the Gaels to Ireland, according to the *Book of Invasions*. As they landed he sang a cosmic hymn in which he identified himself with all creation. Galvin is here generalizing him and his son into a fluid symbol of imagination and resistance.

'Gill Abbey Rock': Finbarr was said to have been buried at Gill Abbey Rock in a silver coffin which was stolen during the Viking invasions. Also site of a foundation of the Augustinian Canons established in 1134.

'Mass of the Lances': A traditional Mass associated with the penal times.

'MacCarthy': A great Munster dynastic family, celebrated by, among others, the poet Aogán Ó Rathaille (?1670–1729).

'Casting my dart': Every May the Mayor of Cork is rowed into Cork Harbour beyond Blackrock Castle and throws a dart into the water to symbolize command of the port.

'Warbeck': Perkin Warbeck (?1474–99), pretender to the throne of Henry VII, landed in Cork where he found support, which is why Cork is known as the 'Rebel City'. After abortive invasions of England he was executed at Tyburn in London.

'O'Sullivan Beare': Muircheartach Óg Ó Súilleabháin (Murty Oge O'Sullivan) of Berehaven, Co. Cork, recruited men for the Irish Brigades on the continent in the eighteenth century. A certain Puxley informed on him; O'Sullivan shot the informer but the authorities killed him in turn after laying siege to his house at Dunboy. They tied the body to a boat and dragged it through the sea to Cork.

'Shannon': Rivers in Irish mythology are associated with tutelary goddesses of place and sovereignty.

'Aideen': In the early Irish tale *Tochmarc Étaíne* (The Wooing of Aideen), the heroine is transformed by witchcraft into a fly which is swallowed by the wife of the king of Ulster who then gives birth to her again. Galvin is loosely adapting the story to his own prophetic mood.

'Red Abbey': Medieval monastery in Cork city, founded *c.*1300 by the Augustinian friars, where they remained until 1641.

'Bridget': A national patron saint who originated as a mythological figure, later Christianized. Her cult was associated with the prestigious monastery at Kildare.

from Roxy's

'This sequence of poems was conceived as a kind of working-class ballet.' (*Interviews*). Roxy's is based on Katie Barry's: see note to 'Statement on the Burning of Cork', p. 73. 'Taken overall, this poem is about the abuse of power.' (*Interviews*). The 'Kings' and 'Queens' are symbols of perverted authority, but they also carry a charge of energy.

Prologue

'Marsh': Slum area of Cork, which gave its name to the city, 'corcach' meaning 'marsh'.

'Connie gate': 'Connie' is a slang term in Cork for the Presentation Convent in Douglas Street.

2 First Confession

'gish': Hiberno-English for a girl, from Irish 'girseach'.

'maw': Hiberno-English for a blow or strike; cf. maul.

4 Lackery

'scrump': Cider.

5 Remember the Night

A parody and burlesque of traditional Irish love song based on 'An chuimhin leat an oíche úd?', a famous love song collected by George Petrie in his *Ancient Music of Ireland* (1855–82), who had it from the Gaelic scholar Eugene O'Curry from Co. Clare.

7 *The Kings are Out*

'Ireland Rising Liberty Street': Now known as Libery Street, but it still has an old street sign which reads 'Ireland's Rising Liberty Street 1798'.

Christ in London

Written in London during the late 1950s, a time of racial tension, reflected in rioting in Notting Hill Gate; also a time of increasing global anxiety caused by the Cold War and the nuclear arms race. The poem was scheduled for broadcast on George MacBeth's BBC radio programme, 'Poetry Now', but it was withheld at first for fear it would be too controversial.

An Caisideach Bán

Tomás Ó Caiside, an eighteenth-century Roscommon poet and Augustinian friar, seems to have been defrocked because of a casual love affair with a young girl. A group of love songs grew up around this tale of love between a woman and her confessor.

The White Monument

Situated at the intersection of Cork's South Mall and Grand Parade, it commemorates the 1798 United Irishmen's Rebellion, the Young Irelanders of the 1840s and the Fenians of the 1860s. The poem is an elegy for Michael Collins (1890–1922), revolutionary and republican, who became director of intelligence in the IRA during the Anglo-Irish War of 1919–22, and then joined the delegation in negotiating the Treaty in London. He took command of the Free State forces in the Civil War and was killed in an ambush at Béal na Bláth, Co. Cork, in 1922. He was known as 'The Big Fella'.

'Deadhouse': Cork *patois* for mortuary.

'Union Gate': The Irish Poor Law Commission in the 1830s divided the country into 130 Unions, each of which administered the local workhouse for the poor. The Cork workhouse was known as 'The Union' and was situated on the site of the present St Finbarr's Hospital, Douglas Road.

Madasha

Part parody, part homage to the 'Celtic Twilight' poetry of the 1890s and the 1900s in Ireland practised by the young W.B. Yeats, George Russell ('AE'), James Cousins and others. The poetry of the Celtic Twilight drew upon Indian themes and philosophy, reflected in Yeats's early Indian poems and Russell's visionary mysticism. This orientalism is evident in Galvin's title, but India had its own magic for him in view of his father's experiences there. See note to 'Plaisir d'Amour', p. 44. The title also refers to the 'Black Ash' ('de Asha'), a wooded, swampy area to the south of Cork now developed as part of the bypass system round the city; it was a place of adventure in Galvin's childhood, with rumours of ghosts and hauntings.

A Day of Rebellion

Excluded by the publishers of Galvin's selected poems, *Man on the Porch* (1979), on the grounds that 'it was a point of view . . . which hadn't been taken up to then . . . and which would cause a lot of controversy' (*Interviews*). The poem is ambivalent towards the 1916 Rising and laments how 'most of the dreams of those who rebelled have never been realized'. The italicized sections are extracts from or adaptations of the Proclamation of the Irish Republic read by Patrick Pearse on Easter Monday 1916.

'Parnell's . . .': Charles Stewart Parnell (1846–91), nationalist leader, MP for Meath (1875) and Cork city (1880). He formed an alliance with the Fenians and became president of the Land League (1879). He led the Irish Parliamentary Party and pressed for Home Rule. He was destroyed by his citation as co-respondent in the O'Shea divorce petition of December 1889.

'O'Leary's ghost in Sackville Street': John O'Leary (1830–1907), Fenian. He served nine years in prison for treason. On his release he influenced W.B. Yeats and Maud Gonne. Sackville Street is now O'Connell Street.

'Fionn and Cúchulain': Fionn Mac Cumhaill and Cú Chulainn are heroic figures of Irish legend and myth.

'Pearse': Patrick Pearse (1879–1916), revolutionary, he led the Easter Rising after a career as an Irish language activist and educationalist, and was executed by a British firing squad.

'mott': Hiberno-English for girl.

'Connolly's . . .': James Connolly (1868–1916), socialist revolutionary. He was a union organizer in Dublin and Belfast before forming the Irish Citizen Army in 1913 to protect workers' rights. In the 1916 Rising he was made commander of the republican forces in Dublin, acting from the headquarters at the GPO. He was executed strapped to a chair because of wounds sustained in the fighting.

'Albion's . . .': Traditional name for England, much used by the poet William Blake, whose phrasing is echoed here.

'Sixteen Dead Men': Title of a poem by Yeats on the executed leaders of the Rising, and of a popular sea-shanty.

Chicken Coop

A poem inspired by the condition of Hungary after it had been taken over by the communists following a rigged election in 1949. Supported by Stalin in Russia, Martyas Rakosi turned upon the nationalist wing of his Workers' Party and executed its leader, Laszlo Rajk. Rakosi exercised absolute control until Stalin's death in 1953. The opening lines mimic the beginning of James Joyce's *A Portrait of the Artist as a Young Man* (1916).

'the McGrath whippet': 'Master McGrath', well-known racing greyhound.

'And the drunken Hamlet . . . reason is the question': Reference to Hamlet's famous soliloquy.